MAKING THE *Eucharist* MATTER

MAKING THE *Eucharist* MATTER

Frank Andersen, M.S.C.

ave maria press Notre Dame, IN

Acknowledgements
Excerpts from ***The New Jerusalem Bible***, copyright © 1985 by Darton, Longman & Todd, Ltd., and Doubleday & Company, Inc., a division of Bantam Doubleday Dell Publishing Group, Inc. Reprinted by permission.

First published 1998, published in the U.S. in 1999 by Ave Maria Press, Inc. by arrangement with John Garratt Publishing, Mulgrave, Australia.
Edited by Kevin Mark Editorial and Literary Services
Typesetting by Bloomfield Advertising
Cover design by Brian C. Conley
Cover photography by CLEO Photography
Printed in the United States of America

Library of Congress Cataloging-in-Publication Data
Andersen Frank.
Making the Eucharist matter / Frank Andersen.
p. cm.
Originally published: Eucharist. Australia : J. Garratt Pub., 1998.
Includes bibliographical references.
ISBN 0-87793-695-1 (pbk.)
1. Mass—Celebration. 2. Lord's Supper—Biblical teaching.
I. Title.
BX2230.2.A63 1999
264'.0203—dc21

99-37728
CIP

CONTENTS

For my father, who so loved his Mass.
Can one ever fully know how profoundly
one's faith is inherited?

PREFACE

To talk about the Eucharist is to talk about the Church. Our inner sense of the Church and of what we imagine the Church to be about can be gathered from the way we find ourselves doing—and speaking about—the Eucharist. The eucharistic life is what the Church is all about. To speak of one is to speak of the other.

The Church is traveling through hard times. Increasing numbers of otherwise faithful Catholics are deserting the Sunday Eucharist or are attending it only irregularly—something unimaginable in our recent past. History tells us that whenever the celebration of the Sunday Eucharist begins to lose its meaning, when going to Mass on Sunday begins to lose its appeal for Catholics, then to that same degree do we begin to lose our sense of being Church.

In short, when Catholics grow uncertain of the Eucharist, their sense of identity is shaken. For attendance at the Eucharist is not just a sign of our attachment to the Church: it is how we *are* Church. One cannot have Catholic faith without a strong commitment to that faith's deepest expression—the Eucharist.

There is something seriously wrong when the joyful celebration of the Sunday Eucharist is no longer the high point of Catholic living. Sadly, can it be said for fewer and fewer Catholics that the Eucharist is *the source* and *the summit* of their life in the Church (cf. Vatican II's *Constitution on the Liturgy*, no. 10, and *Dogmatic Constitution on the Church*, no. 11).

Personally, these times have proved the most challenging of my fifty or so years of faith. It is as if Vatican II's liturgical renewal—begun in the 1960s—is only now impacting in its seriousness of endeavor; that only now are we realizing the full extent of the conversion required if Catholicism is to speak words of hope and meaning to the people of this age. The change of attitude facing us is more profound than we have realized. Conversion (once seen as what happened to others) is now the task to be faced within our own Catholic hearts and minds, something for the Church itself.

The need to rework our faith's expression into a language appropriate for today's world is not only a difficult task, but one that remains largely still to be done. Like the apostles at Pentecost, we need again to learn "the languages of the world" if the gospel of the Lord is to be set free and rendered effective.

Despite the best of intentions and the hard work of many, the majority of people in Sunday congregations are not particularly involved in the ritual that is going on around them. It is as if they are no longer sure of what it is that the ritual is trying to achieve—as if they do not quite know why they are there. Many have a vague uneasiness that something crucial is amiss and that somehow they have managed to lose the *connection to mystery* that lies at the heart of the sacrament.

This book concerns that connection to mystery. In this sense, I trust it is an endeavor faithful to those earlier generations of Catholics for whom the Mass was replete with its own sense of mystery. I myself have lived almost half my life in that older, now passing Church, and value the commitment in faith that I absorbed from those around me. I have lived in times of faith vastly different from now. I have been fortunate to have lived in what can sometimes be seen as almost two distinct and different Churches—then and now.

Studies at the Pontifical Liturgical Institute in Rome grounded me in the historical dimensions of Church life, confirming that it is of the very nature of this Church to be always on a journey, continually making its way through history and amongst differing generations. At times we have camped in strange forests, feeding our theological campfires with whatever timbers were locally available at the time. But when we move further along down the road, the timbers of past fires provide little warmth and comfort. My early years were spent in an encampment that had lasted four hundred years, since the Council of Trent. I was nourished and warmed by the terminology of the Middle Ages: transubstantiation, host and sacrifice, body and blood, soul and divinity. I do not doubt for one moment the truths they were attempts to express; but I doubt the cogency of such language for many of today's congregations.

Herein lies the nub of this book: in terms of a language for faith, we find ourselves in a moment of history that can only be described as one of *transition*. Let me declare from the outset that I see myself *building upon* the understandings that nourished my earlier Catholic years—not replacing those understandings. The tradition we knew as coming from Trent has been broadened by the Church itself into areas of community participation that are already far beyond the Mass-going experience of my childhood years. This book will explore those deeper dimensions of participation that lie at the heart of the Christian eucharistic liturgy. We have always claimed that the Eucharist is the unique sacrifice of Christ; but what I wish to explore here is the manner in which that crucial belief has meaning *for us*, how it implicates *us*, how it ennobles and involves *us*. Nothing less than the future of Catholic liturgy depends on how clearly we come to see the Eucharist's relevance for *our* lives.

The Eucharist has always been at the heart of my faith and remains so. In a similar vein, the Real Presence of Jesus in the sacrament is precious to me, but there are levels of appreciating its meaning—and our involvement in its meaning—that eluded me in my younger years. Catholicism's boast is its sacramental system, but what we had lost sight of was the very nature of a *sacrament*. Unable to participate—and trading sacrament for literalism—we settled for being an audience at Mass. This loss of a sense of ritual was not merely a Catholic problem. Carl Jung was right: the Western mind had lost touch with symbolic thinking, and the rituals of faith (our sacraments) were losing their relevance for our lives. This is called a crisis of faith. Unable to experience their lives as *part of the mystery* of Jesus, so many no longer walk—or worship—with us today.

In times of disorientation and uncertainty over the direction of our travel, we refer more carefully to our original directions: we return to our origins.

This book inspects the rituals and symbols of the Eucharist, not with the theological tools and language of the Middle Ages, but by returning to the scriptures about Jesus. Much of what follows is owed almost entirely to the scholarship and fine teaching of the Benedictines at San Anselmo in Rome. They opened for me those lengthier traditions that reached back into the culture that gave birth to Jesus. They embodied the best of the Roman mind, which sees the pastoral, prudent adaptation of ritual to the needs of differing cultures as a clear mark of fidelity to tradition. I take full responsibility, for better or worse, for those parts of the book that arise from my own efforts to apply such learning to the tricky pastoral situations of our culture today and of our struggle to make faith and worship relevant. Despite the protests of many, I maintain that the Church in today's world is still a long way from home. If any of the material in this book promotes a greater clarity about issues basic to our central act of worship—the Eucharist—then it will have contributed in some small way to that long journey home.

Wishing to keep the text clear and readable, I have included non-biblical references and further comments in the endnotes. However, they are an integral part of a serious reading of the book. Also, it should be noted that any emphasis (indicated by italics) that appears in the quotations has been added by me, unless otherwise noted.

The suggestions for discussion at the end of each chapter are intended to deepen the reader's response to the preceding material and to facilitate the text's application to the ritual of the Eucharist. Designed with a view to stimulating group discussion, this material can also be used profitably by a solitary reader. The many discussion points provided will allow parish groups or ministry teams to return more than once for a deepening of a chapter's material. The discussion sections are thus an integral part of the book and a way of working the text deeper into our worship consciousness.

CHAPTER ONE

The Tradition Jesus Inherited

Like a stirring deep within ...

The Eucharist is a human attempt to describe God. It portrays the struggle within all of us between graciousness and meanness, between a vision of what human community can become and a denial of responsibility for one another. The eucharistic ritual is one tradition's response to the search for meaning in human existence. A shape Christians give to God is Eucharist.

While I stress the human dimensions of the Eucharist, I do not wish to suggest that the divine energy of God played no part in its birth, development, and expression. What I am suggesting is that when human beings wrestle with issues such as freedom and servitude, suffering and compassion, and generosity, self-giving and community, then it is truly the *divine-within-us* that so struggles and writhes. I wish to intimate that God is *emerging* in human history—whether we like it or not—and that this is what religion is about. Christians call that struggle Jesus, or faith, or Eucharist. God's Spirit yearns to take human shape; humanity's hope is to be caught up totally in the divine. In the person we call Jesus, these two coalesce: fully human, yet we name him divine—the unique, total articulation of divine life, and of human life. His is the story of God's Spirit: that character so deeply embedded within us as to constitute our very souls. We are created "in the image and likeness" of God (Genesis 1:27).

At birth, no one of us possesses in full this divine "image and likeness," but we do carry the seed. Our response to life is the nurturing of this seed (or, sadly, its diminishment). Human lives, maturing lovingly, create God's presence on earth and thus bring creation to its fulfilment—in a real sense we render God visible. To be collaborators with God in this intimate way is our deepest ennoblement. It constitutes our graciousness. Yet it is a fashioning never completed, a consciousness never fully obtained.

To misread this profound sense of human dignity, to live in ways destructive of the human spirit or disfiguring of creation's intense beauty is to sin.

Viewing God and ourselves in this way has deep and serious implications for how we understand Jesus. The Eucharist commemorates *his* total engagement in that struggle, his *commitment* to that vision. In him the consciousness was achieved; in him that hoped-for fullness blossomed. We believe him to be the embodiment of God, the transformation of human life. He is rightly the core and fascination of our Christian tradition. We call him the Way and the Truth and the Life (cf. John 14:6).

Who was this human one who, alone of all of us, proved capable of constantly saying "yes" to the promptings of inner Spirit?[2] Who was this simple Galilean peasant who, more than any of us can imagine, so lived that divine Spirit's tenderness, beauty, and proximity as to become known by those who follow him as the Son of God? Who was this Jewish one who dared to call God *Abba* and of whom we sing each morning: "You have raised up Jesus from the servant House of David..."?[3]

Was Jesus truly raised from within the servant House of David? Do we really believe he was truly, inherently Jewish? Do we honestly commit ourselves to the belief that it was within the struggle and beauty of Jewish tradition that he was nurtured, fashioned, and formed? And what implications flow from the assertion that he took to himself "descent from Abraham" (Hebrews 2:16)?

The perspective of this book is that Jesus was precisely this: the offspring of a struggling and heroically faithful people, and that in him—bone of their bone and blood of their blood—the tradition of this extraordinary Hebrew nation reached its greatest reality in the flesh of one of their own. In short, that Jesus inherited their vision-for-life and that he saw himself as part of their timeless quest to "pass over" into God. Jesus was part of a nation who saw themselves called to become God's *Passover people*.

This quest to be the embodiment of God's fidelity was grounded for the Hebrew people in an abiding and sharp *memory* of their origins and history. For them—and for Jesus—faith meant a commitment to the hard-won insights of the past as well as a loyalty to real people within their all-too-real history: "True to what was promised through our spirit-filled ancestors ..." [4]

This sense of human continuity is crucial to the Hebrew mind. Their faith has always been down-to-earth. Suffering, struggle, and failure have been the fabric of their history, fashioning their identity. This is a people who have used religious rituals to focus their national memory, knowing from sad experience that in forgetting its past a nation loses its inner root and wisdom. Festivals and religious celebrations give shape and form to such wisdoms as their ancestors had learned, becoming opportunities to keep themselves *mindful* of who they are before God, preserving the consciousness of their traditions and national commitments. In such rituals they continually name themselves as part of an historical development: called to be *God's* People! They see themselves as God's *holy* Nation whose story began with Abraham and Moses in the distant origins of their history.

Within that process of remembered history, one moment, one encounter with Mystery stood high above all else in constituting them as a nation. This one event—both painful and glorious—fashioned their vision and identity and set them on a quest for what they saw—from that moment—to be the heart and purpose of their existence. In their language it is called *Passover*. When the books of the Bible were translated into Greek, it became *Exodus*.[5]

The two words—Passover and Exodus—refer to a real happening, an escape from Egypt across the Red Sea, through the desert, and finally into possession of their own land. They physically *passed over* into freedom, while at the same time *passing over* from being a loose rabble of separate families and tribes into a unified nation. Both meanings are important.

It was an inspiring transition: into a new consciousness, a new sense of identity, an expansion of the horizons of the mind toward *inclusivity*, changing the boundaries that separated tribe from tribe. Today, as contemporary symbols of human destiny, Exodus and

Passover are terms that still function: expressing how we might move (in these times) from disparate, isolated nations toward global community in a new human *ex-odus*; how we might *pass-over*—yet again—into a new dimension of international consciousness and responsibility.

We cannot overstate the importance of this image of Passover. The Gospels present the life of Jesus as culminating in that image. John, particularly, even plays upon the image of journey when introducing the Last Supper of Jesus:

> Before the festival of the Passover, Jesus, knowing that his hour had come *to pass from this world to the Father* ... (John 13:1) [6]

What then, was this mentality—inherited by Jesus—by which the Hebrews called themselves God's Passover People? We return to the book of Exodus to uncover the Hebrew roots of the mindset and ritual that would blossom on the night of the Last Supper. Without a clear perception of where Passover all began, we will never begin to appreciate what Jesus thought he was doing on that final evening of his life.

Exodus and Passover

The Hebrews called themselves a "Passover People" and the great event of their Exodus from Egypt was the moment in which they became conscious of this calling.

It would be hard to overestimate the intense suffering that gave birth to the nation called Israel. The tradition out of which our Eucharist would come was born in pain.

It would be no exaggeration to suggest that our Hebrew ancestors in faith found holocaust a familiar traveler throughout their history: firstly, their enslavement in Egypt, later their deportation as a nation to exile in Babylon. In our century we have slowly accepted the uncomfortable truth of the European holocaust, those Christian-led pogroms of the Middle Ages that culminated in the horrors of Auschwitz.

But let us not allow these momentous events to minimize Israel's recurring experiences of foreign invasion throughout history, this unhappily situated land bridged between East and West. Even during the time of Jesus, the country was under an oppressive Roman military occupation with its all too frequent brutalities against the people. Israel is a nation familiar with terror.

Enslaved in Egypt, the Hebrew people's suffering is difficult to imagine if one's own country has not experienced similar humiliation and degradation. Oppressed and abused by foreigners, alienated from the comforts of their own cultural practices, and marginalized as slaves, their loss of self-identity was profound. Perhaps there are some within our contemporary experiences of nationhood who have tasted what this means, but for many of us genocide and enslavement are simply words on a page. Hebrew poets of a later (but similar) experience would sing:

> By the rivers of Babylon,
> there we sat and we wept ...
> When we remembered our country,
> there we sat and we wept ...[7]

Unable to endure such suffering, the Hebrew people eventually break out into the wilderness of Sinai. Moses is named as their leader, but what really drives them into Exodus (and would later drive Jesus himself out into the wilderness) is that inner Spirit of God, common to us all, but now rebellious and angry under oppression.

Inspired by Moses, they pay attention to those irrepressible, inner yearnings for freedom—and surely this is an important aspect of what Christians mean by the restless Spirit of God. Courageously attentive to their heart's longings they dared the dangerous path of breaking-out into the wilderness: allowing the Spirit to lead them into ways as yet unknown. Within this story there are several levels of meaning to the terms *transition* or *pass-over*.

1. Leaving Egypt, daring the wilderness, they eventually enter God's Promised Land. On face value, this is an incredible story

of physical hardship and homelessness: a *geographical transition* from one country to another.

2. At another level, during this geographical transition, a collection of tribes becomes welded into a new identity: the community of God's People. They become a nation: they undergo a *social transition* from being a fragmented people into becoming a community.
3. At still another level, they mature from the suffering and anger of their enslavement in Egypt into a new understanding of peace and a sense of compassion that gives birth to new community: a *moral transition*. This aspect of *pass-over* is never-ending—it challenges humanity still. The Gospel word for this reshaping of the human mind is *conversion*.

This third level of meaning is the sense of pass-over on which we will concentrate. Although guided by an ever-prayerful Moses, this growth into national and spiritual maturity was ignited by the people's sufferings in Egypt. We must never lose sight of the role anguish plays in the origins of our faith vision.

When human beings are violated, crushed, or exploited, two responses are possible:

1. The first is a response of *violence*, fuelled by anger and unjust suffering. The heart, turned in on its own hurt, is closed; the capacity to love is not enlarged. Conscious only of one's own pain, violence is inflicted upon another. The cycle of human violation is perpetuated.
2. The second is a response of *compassion*, fuelled by the same anger and sense of injustice. But now the heart, wounded and made wise to the inhumanity of injustice, is opened; the capacity to love is enlarged. Knowing suffering, one learns the taste of the sufferings of others. Violence blossoms into compassion and understanding.

Human beings, when victimized by oppression, are moved (or choose to move) into one or other of these two responses. There is no middle or neutral course. On one path lies the way of personal (and community) greatness; on the other, personal (and community) disintegration. The story of Exodus charts the magnificent response of the long-suffering people of Israel. In their challenging turn-around lies the seed of what Jesus would do on the final night of his life at the Last Supper.

The Covenant Vision

The Hebrew people emerged from enslavement in Egypt to fashion for themselves a vision of what their community could become. This was their greatness: out of suffering they emerge with hope: a hope to which they gave practical shape. Its specific name is *covenant*.[8]

For in the wilderness of Sinai, the people "meet their God" and in that engagement they commit themselves to a noble ideal. Now, for the first time in their history, free to make choices about the shape of their own future, they realize their capacity to craft their own form of society. Matured in the cauldron of suffering, these survivors will courageously construct together *a new nation* and collaborate in fashioning something never before known on earth: a society of justice and mercy. But not just any justice, nor just any mercy. Their nation would reflect in its structures and lifestyle the same justice and mercy that they themselves had experienced in the loving fidelity of the God they had come to know. Theirs would be a nation in which *no one, however insignificant, would endure anything of the alienation and suffering which they themselves knew only too well from enslavement in Egypt.*

Suffering had opened their eyes and hearts. In the wilderness of their life's tragic experience, they had truly "met God" in a way they had never known before. What they had met, of course, were the deepest longings of their hearts for justice and mercy. Their inborn image of God had, in suffering, been deeply affronted. Their years of slavery were their wilderness, long before their entry into the wastelands of Sinai. In Hebrew symbolism the wilderness is a privileged place for the encounter between God and ourselves.

We need to be realistic about what is going on here. How is it—in the best of Hebrew tradition—that human beings actually "meet God"? Let us examine closely the wilderness image as we find it in Exodus.

The way the story tells it, God calls to Moses and invites him to climb the mountain. There, on the mountain, Moses speaks and listens to God's demands. Moses then returns to the people waiting on the plains below and informs them of God's commands. The people respond and Moses conveys their acceptance back to the mountaintop God.

In such a portrayal, God is imagined almost in human form and as relating to Moses—and the less worthy people below—in ways familiar to us from human interaction. In this use of the story form, God is presented as a person who comes to the mountain, who calls, who speaks, who bargains, and who waits to hear the outcome.

It helps to realize that such important moments in Israel's journey needed to be told orally (as stories long cherished and well remembered) around the campfires, centuries before they were ever put into writing. Destined never to be forgotten, such stories needed to be graphic, easy to memorize, and dramatic for impact. Much oral tradition lies underneath these ancient, written stories of a nation's past.

But what might have been the reality?

Some clue might be taken from that most Hebrew of Gospel stories that we once called the story of the Prodigal Son. It is more accurately named these days as the story of the Loving Father.

In that beautifully crafted story of Luke 15, once the younger son has gone to a foreign land and there wasted his father's money, he finds himself derelict and in a pigsty. For a Jewish listener, this is the ultimate humiliation: a degrading loss of identity not unlike what their nation had experienced in Egypt.

Now one could say that in his moment of degradation, God spoke to the young man, making him remember his father. But what is actually mentioned as happening? The translation that many of us have long since memorized, says: "Then he came to his senses ... " (Luke 15:16).

There is something disturbingly normal about these beautiful words: by what common, everyday process does the Spirit of

God attempt to engage our consciousness? The promptings of the irrepressible Spirit, deep within our being, are the source of all wisdom and insight. The key is to be attentive and to notice the stirrings. When the Church speaks of prayer, this is what the best of Christian tradition always has in mind: the art of *listening*, of *noticing* what is occurring within our lives and being.

The beauty of this Hebrew nation—broken and afraid as they enter the wilderness of Sinai—is that, like the prodigal son in failure, they too "come to their senses." They listen to their heart's experience of violation and oppression. They are educated "in the school of suffering"[9] and their wisdom gives rise to a noble vision. Under the leadership of Moses they accepted that inner invitation to choose the way of compassion and justice. In this precise sense, God *offers them* a covenant. They will commit themselves to the better path and build together a nation embodying their hard-learned wisdom. No ordinary society, this! It will be characterized by a specific set of regulations and shared commitments, all designed with a view to the respectful and tender treatment of all. We know these regulations as the Ten Commandments.

From our childhood we are familiar with the Ten Commandments; we are not as familiar with the covenant of which they form the heart and soul. Without a clearer grasp of the covenant fashioned by this unusual people, we will never understand the soil and roots of our Eucharist.

Let us now look more closely at the text of the book of Exodus where this process of making covenant is portrayed:

> Moses then went up to God, and Yahweh called to him …
>
> "You have seen for yourselves what I did to the Egyptians and how I carried you away on eagle's wings and brought you to me. So now, if you are really prepared to *obey me* and *keep my covenant*, you out of all peoples, shall be my personal possession, for the whole world is mine. For me you shall be a kingdom of priests, a holy nation." [10]

> So Moses went and summoned the people's elders and acquainted them with everything that Yahweh had bidden him, and the people all replied with one accord:
>
> *"Whatever Yahweh has said, we will do."* (Exodus 19:3-8)

Notice here the centrality of obedience: "If you *obey* me ... you shall be my personal possession."

To become God's treasured possession is totally dependent on the people's *obedience* to what God asks. Obedience is the single, total yardstick of closeness to this God. In Hebrew and Christian tradition, the core of all religion is *obedience* to God's promptings.

Here also is portrayed one of the most important aspects of the liturgy we have inherited from the Hebrew tradition: "And the people all replied with one accord ... " We will return to this later, but let us note here the process of proclamation and response that provides the fundamental dynamic of all good liturgy. A challenging vision is thrown to the people (proclamation) who in turn—and in one voice—throw it right back (response) with: "Yes!" The responsive nature of Christian liturgy comes from this deeply Hebrew tradition: our rituals are participative in their very origin. And the response must come from the *whole* congregation.

This captivating interaction between God, Moses, and the people of Israel occurs in the nineteenth chapter of Exodus. This is the first time that Moses puts to the people "everything that Yahweh had bidden him." They respond positively to the vision.

In Exodus chapter 20 we are presented with the Decalogue itself, the Ten Commandments. In this chapter we find them presented in an abbreviated, easily memorized form (much as we ourselves learned them as children). Although abbreviated, they catch the essence of what God is asking of them, but the detail—as it were—is found in the fine print of the following three chapters! There we find an exposition of these "ten commandments" in terms of how they impact on all the different strata of social life in this proposed new nation:

- Attitudes to the deity, to slaves, toward life and creation, and to resolving quarrels (chapter 21).
- Attitudes toward the possessions of others, toward foreigners, the poor, and between families (chapter 22).
- Issues relating to maliciousness, keeping festivals and the Sabbath, of justice toward all, including a certain basic justice toward enemies (chapter 23).

Let us not misunderstand the point and purpose of the Decalogue. In this presentation the Commandments are no mere personal morality—as we perhaps imbibed them in our younger days. Crafted in this careful fashion, these chapters form a *political platform*, a vision for the formation of a nation, a *corporate consensus* that governs all relationships within society—relationships to God, one's parents, the rich, the poor, strangers, even enemies.[11] In terms of relationships, justice was the issue: a justice modeled on God's loyalty and tenderness for themselves in escaping the holocaust that was Egypt.

The Commandments speak of "God's justice"—not "justice" in our Western, European sense of courtroom justice, of getting what one's actions deserve. No, Hebrew tradition sees the "justice of God" as something critically different and ennobling: God's justice is that enduring attitude of loving tenderness that constantly affirms the dignity and sacredness of all. It shows itself in endless patience, in boundless compassion, and in rock-like solidarity in love. To miss this astonishing aspect of the word "justice" in the religious language of Israel is to miss the heart and soul of their entire faith.

And so it was that around the term "justice" there arose this comprehensive vision for the formation of a *new national identity*—and a *social expression of that identity*—so unique that even "outsiders" could not but be impressed! Justice and peace have embraced in *this* nation. No ordinary people this—their social structure embodies the very character of their God. This nation, with its compelling vision of merciful concern for all, would be like a light to all nations of how humanity could live together in peace and harmony.

It is precisely in this commitment to justice for all that the true *exodus* is found, the *true transition.* To the best of their ability they would choose to express in their lives the tender mercy of God. Exodus tells the story of a passover from a people they *once were* into a People they *could be.* It was a quest that would never end, a hunger never to be satisfied, but they were inspired by a vision born in the crucible of human suffering and desperation. To actually live this vision of community, to guarantee a society in which all experienced and exercised their true dignity, this is what it would mean to "pass-over" into God's "land" of freedom and peace.

The covenant was a national commitment never to be forgotten. The different rituals of Israel's religious life were simply attempts to ensure that the commitment was always prominent in their memories.

The Covenant Liturgy

They would commit themselves to this covenant. They would attempt that most painful of tasks: to learn to collaborate as a nation. We now find described in chapter 24 of Exodus a foundational liturgy that we must study with care. Its relationship, not only to what Jesus did on the night before he died, but also to our own eucharistic struggle in these final years of the twentieth century, will be evident. I take the liberty to highlight three components that are of central importance if we are to understand what we are trying to do at the Eucharist.

But first, an introductory piece that sets the scene for this great liturgy of the people:

> Moses put all Yahweh's words into writing, and early next morning he *built an altar* at the foot of the mountain, with *twelve standing-stones* for *the twelve tribes of Israel.* Then he sent certain young Israelites to offer burnt offerings and sacrifice bullocks to Yahweh as *communion sacrifices.* (Exodus 24:4-5)

Two comments are immediately apparent. Firstly, Moses is attempting to communicate with the total nation: the twelve standing-stones. Secondly, Moses is attempting to express something important about what it means to come into communion with God: the setting is a *communion sacrifice.*

Moses is probing what it meant for the nation to be in communion with God. Unlike ourselves, for whom Holy Communion has become an *individual* experience, the essence of Hebrew tradition is that communion with God is something *communal.* Their culture (unlike ours) possessed an innate grasp of what the Greek language would later call liturgy: that is, a ritual by means of which a community—or, in their case, a whole nation—could express for itself the sort of community it wished to be.[12]

For this primitive people—and I use the word in its best sense—the power of this liturgical activity is majestic. What Moses is attempting to say is far beyond human words, so he does what all of us do when words fail our need to communicate at depth and with urgency: he acts out a *symbolism.*[13]

The genius of all liturgy is precisely this, that symbols provide a language when language itself can no longer function.

Moses' symbol is graphic: he makes use of blood. The very sight of blood (or its smell, or even its mention) immediately conjures up two related but opposing images: life and death. Deep in the recesses of the human psyche, blood is about *life* and *death*. Moses is trying to say something of great moment to his people, something about issues of life and death. To do so, he needs blood (hence the killing of the bullocks).

As the liturgy of Moses continues, let me present the first component of their celebration. Having killed some bullocks to collect their blood, what does Moses now do with it? Firstly:

> Moses then took half the blood and put it into basins, and the other half he sprinkled on the altar. (Exodus 24:6)

He collects half of the blood and puts it to the side for the moment. The other half he sprinkles over "the altar" that stands in the center of "the twelve tribes."

Not a word is spoken. It is all done in silence. In a culture close to the earth and still fluent in the language of symbol, words are not needed.

Blood on the altar. Sacred life. God's life. The only life we associate with altars. God's blood. The onlookers sense the awesomeness of what Moses is struggling to articulate. How he focuses their attention, this masterly communicator! Attuned to the meanings of blood, they are totally attentive to the dimensions of his powerful gesture.

Moses pauses ...

> Then, taking the Book of the Covenant, he read it to *the listening people*, who then said, "We shall do everything that Yahweh has said; *we shall obey.*" (Exodus 24:7)

In the pause, Moses takes up the book that outlines the relationships of justice they would live: he proclaims to the listening people this newly crafted *constitution* for a society never before seen on earth. He challenges them with the detail of their commitment, confronts them verbally with the insights of their own wisdom, the implications of their own hard-won compassion: *Will they become this sort of nation?*

They listen. They take to heart this confronting proclamation. They rise *as one* to this dangerous perspective of living more nobly and *in one voice* declare: "We shall do everything that Yahweh has said; *we shall obey.*"

Now the liturgy can continue ...

For it is only then, once the people have given their assent to the vision portrayed in the proclamation of the covenant, once they have thereby agreed to what its embodiment will cost them—only then—does Moses complete the symbolic gesture: he sprinkles the people with the *same blood*, the *same life*, as was previously spread over the altar, on God.

> Moses then took *the blood* [saved in the basins] and sprinkled it over the people, saying, "*This is the blood of the*

> *covenant* which Yahweh has made with you, *entailing all these stipulations*." (Exodus 24:8)

The symbolism is brilliant: God's life = their life. But only *if* they obey the vision, only *if* they agree to embody the covenant. It is important to notice the centrality of God's Word in all this: it is their commitment to the Word that makes them a community, so much so that *without the Word of God there is no commonality with God.*

This text is lucid: the life that anoints God (the altar) is the same life anointing them (the people)—*but only to the degree that they obey!*

In case there is the slightest doubt about the symbolic meaning of "the blood" in this celebration, Moses exclaims as he casts it over the people:

> "This is the blood of the covenant which Yahweh has made with you, entailing all these stipulations."

Notice that this liturgy speaks not merely of "communion with God." Clearly implied in communion with God is the deliberate intention to *express together God's justice:* human community is integral to divine communion. There is no sense here of individually receiving God's presence. Communion with God—in Hebrew tradition—is achieved in the shared task of fashioning just human community.

This insight into the meaning of communion with God may come as a shock to those of us brought up on Holy Communion as one's private, personal experience of intimacy with Jesus. But this very individualism is itself the difficulty. The genius of our Hebrew ancestors was to recognize that God's face is shown forth in compassionate community—a tradition inherited and lived by Jesus. Questioned by a Pharisee, Jesus stands firmly in the tradition of the covenant when he replies:

> "You must love the Lord your God with all your heart, with all your soul, and with all your mind. This is the greatest and

the first commandment. *The second resembles it:* You must *love your neighbor* as yourself. On these two commandments hang the *whole Law* ..." (Matthew 22:37-40)

Drinking from the Chalice

When we celebrate the Eucharist today, what does it mean to drink the Blood of Christ?[14]

Indeed, for Catholics, this is a question that has only arisen in recent times: within our living memories, the sharing of the chalice was simply not done. Prior to the Vatican II reform, only the priest drank from the chalice. Perhaps even more disturbing is the fact that despite the opportunity for all communicants to do so now, it is a practice laboring under real difficulties:

1. Many communicants, comfortable receiving the eucharistic bread, choose *not to share* the cup;
2. Of those who do receive from the cup, some prefer *not to drink*, but rather to dip the host into the cup ("intinction");
3. Few communicants, in either camp, would have a clear grasp of what "drinking the Blood of Christ" actually *means*.

For a range of reasons, therefore, we are prepared "to eat" but not as ready "to drink" when it comes to Holy Communion. This split in our practice of the sacrament should of itself alert us to the fact that something momentous is missing from our understanding of the wholeness of the Mystery.

Our split practice concerning the reception of the Eucharist is historical as much as theological. Few would realize that only in this century have we seen the return of congregations to the practice of frequent Communion. Pope St. Pius X, often remembered as the pope who lowered the age of children's First Communion to around the age of seven years, was actually more notable for his policies of encouraging the return of *adult* Catholics to more frequent reception of the Eucharist. The rise of the Holy Name Society (men) and the Sacred Heart Sodality (women) in the first half of this century were deliberate, papal-led attempts to encourage regular (monthly) reception of the Eucharist. Prior to that time (the early 1900s), few adult Catholics communicated regularly. Since about the fifth century, adult reception of the Eucharist was rare. We do well to keep ourselves in perspective: in terms of historical time, we are currently in a process of eucharistic recovery. While today many will take the eucharistic bread, our attitudes to the cup are not as strong. Even more importantly, our sense of what is signified by the taking of either bread or cup seems far from clear.

We were accustomed, in an earlier time, to view the bread as the person of Jesus and the chalice of blood as in reality no different from that same person. If we received him "in the bread," what more of him was there to receive "in the wine"?

Why, indeed, take both?

In the covenant liturgy of Exodus, the meaning of "the blood" is stark and persuasive. Nor can we dismiss this meaning as something merely of our older Hebrew roots. For there is one line in the above liturgy that the Church has lifted out and placed squarely in the core of *every* eucharistic celebration we attend. I refer to the words of Moses as he sprinkles the people: "This is the blood of the covenant ... " (Exodus 24:8)

The Church has planted this startling text right into the account of the Last Supper, putting these same words onto the lips of Jesus. These words are repeated at every Eucharist, in the moment that we call the consecration. They are the exact same words, slightly altered in form but enormously altered in meaning: "This is the cup of my blood, the blood of the *new* and *everlasting* covenant." [15]

The Gospel accounts of the Last Supper, each in their own way, stress the connection of that night of Jesus' life with the Passover feast. They are making a deliberate connection with the covenant of Exodus.

The Church makes the same connection to this Exodus liturgy in every eucharistic celebration: by lifting the crucial image of blood out of that original covenant ritual to confront every Catholic community with its meaning. It is this image of blood that we have struggled to preserve by insisting on describing the Mass as a *sacrifice*. We must recover the full meanings of blood; just as urgently we must find ways to persuade all participants to participate fully in the eucharistic gesture by drinking from the cup of the blood of Christ.[16]

What primitive meanings of blood lie underneath the rituals of communion used by Moses in the covenant liturgy?

Blood, the word or the reality, immediately confronts us with twinned realizations: *life* and *death*. Beyond the power of words and with intensity, the confrontation blood triggers is profound.

So when we speak of "the blood of Christ" or say that "the death of Jesus" saves us, are we not also suggesting that the way he lived his life saves us? Indeed, in a real sense, the way Jesus lived his life was a constant "death": a generous giving of himself despite the cost so that others might live.

Is it not also our own experience that living and dying are not as dissimilar as the words might indicate? To love is to give; to give with constancy is to die to my own comforts and preferences. Yet such a generous life is also a fulfilment—even, some would say, the enrichment within loving—when we "die" for another in ordinary, everyday ways. This is the meaning of love. In Hebrew culture, the word "blood" catches both dimensions of this mystery by which we all are driven.

When faced with the challenge of the covenant agreement, the people of Israel *listened to the word of God* and courageously gave their assent to work with one another toward its embodiment: they would collaborate in the creation of God's just society. Once they had declared their *obedience* to that proclaimed word, Moses could sprinkle them with the *blood*. It is no different for us in the eucharistic liturgy today.

When gathered for the Eucharist, the first major movement of the celebration is when the people—including presider and ministers—listen to the Word of God. The readings depict for us the demands of God (as did the reading of the commandments at Sinai). In our case, however, the demands of God were lived by a person, Jesus, the new commandment. So Eucharist begins as we listen to stories of how God's justice *actually took shape* in Jesus' life (the Lectionary readings). In the time of Moses, the listening community committed itself to shape something still hoped for; but we (in the time since Jesus) gather each Sunday to remember *a shaping that has already been demonstrated* in his living.

Then, having listened to the Word of God (the living shape that Jesus gave to the covenant), we too dedicate ourselves to embodying that covenant in our own day and circumstance. Like the Hebrews in the wilderness, we commit ourselves to the same vision—except that our name for that vision is Jesus. And the contemporary world is as urgently in need of communities that embody "the saving face of God" as ever were needed in the time of Moses. We listen to the gospel with attention. We then commit ourselves *as one community* to live what we have heard: we will *obey!*

And immediately, on proclaiming our *obedience*, we too can be "sprinkled with the blood." The life of God (the blood of Jesus named at the consecration) is now "sprinkled over" us: and the condition is still *obedience to the Word*.

However, there is one difference: unlike the Hebrews at Sinai, we are not merely sprinkled "on the outside," as it were. For us, the washing with blood is "on the inside," it is our inner being, our spirit, that is committed. Like Ezekiel, we name ourselves as a people of new heart, as communities distinguished by compassion (cf. Ezekiel 36:26).

And so we drink the blood. We take it within ourselves. In an action of profound inner commitment we drink into ourselves the Word of God we have just listened to in the gospel portrayal of Jesus. We drink the story *into* ourselves; we drink ourselves *into* the Story.

As in the original covenant, we thereby commit ourselves *to one another* in the noble, collaborative task of creating on earth a community that embodies the justice of the gospel. We drink—together—from the *one cup* of the blood of the covenant. I watch you drink the commitment. You watch me drink that same commitment. We both are washed in the blood; we stand together. In sharing from the *one* cup (as in sharing of the *one* loaf of bread) something is happening between us. What that "something" is will only be discovered in the doing.

When we participate in a Eucharist today, it is still the Passover that we are attempting. We face today—and just as urgently—the same question that faced the Hebrew people as they came struggling out of Egypt: *How do human beings pass-over into God?* There is no greater religious quest than this.

Just as it is the same question, so it is the same liberating insight: we pass-over into God when we consciously agree *to become the community* that takes on the task of crafting for ourselves and presenting to the world God's *fidelity* and *tender mercy*. The drinking of the blood of Christ seals that communal commitment to live together the pattern of his lifestyle and to fashion our community on the vision that filled him.

Hence, the *two* dimensions of Holy Communion: not only is it our quest to come into communion *with God*; the Hebrew insight was that communion *with one another* is just as important and life-giving. The privilege—and the dangerous challenge—is to live in a holy communion of God's people. In our truest traditions the act of approaching Holy Communion is a declaration of one's total commitment to this struggling, courageous community and to its consciously proclaimed task of living the covenant that was Jesus. For us, Jesus is the covenant in full bloom. There is no other. He alone is the blood of God.

For Discussion

1. The sufferings of Egypt, the covenant vision of the Hebrews in the wilderness, and the Ten Commandments that summarized that vision—all these are closely related.
   What have you learnt in this chapter about these three realities? As Catholics, we would do well to begin talking again in terms of *the covenant*. Perhaps it is a terminology that we have lost—and to our detriment: for in losing the concept of covenant we lose an important part of our roots.
   Discuss.

2. The Eucharist was born in pain and suffering. It will be most appreciated by those who know something of that same struggle within their lives. It has been said that the Eucharist is for *broken people*. Yet the tradition we have inherited would maintain that to communicate within the ritual of the Eucharist, one must be sinless.

Discuss the realities and implications of this for the Church and for ourselves.

3. In the letter to the Hebrews (5:8) it says of Jesus that he "learnt obedience ... through his sufferings."
   The Hebrew vision of covenant—their commitment to obey—was forged in the suffering of Egypt.
   Working together, share and list the various experiences of suffering that you believe the Church is undergoing at this time of its growth.
   What life-giving aspects do you see for the Church in its current struggle, suffering, or "wilderness"?

4. The Word of God (the readings) is seen by many Catholics as of secondary importance to the sacraments of bread and wine. However, from our analysis of the Exodus liturgy, how crucial to sacramental communion is the Word of God? Indeed—according to this tradition which Jesus inherited—can there be Holy Communion without the Word?
   Discuss any new understanding you may have of these issues flowing from this chapter.

5. When speaking of Holy Communion, we commonly use terms like "we receive Jesus."
   What do you imagine most Catholics mean by those words? Or what do you imagine our children take them to mean? Within your lifetime, what change to the meaning of these words have you noticed?
   In the light of the communion liturgy of the covenant of Exodus, what might the words "receive Jesus" truly mean?

6. A eucharistic minister is holding before you the Communion chalice, inviting you with these familiar words: "The Blood of Christ."
   In terms of the covenant liturgy, what precisely is being offered to you? And to what are you agreeing when you respond, "Amen"?

As you take and drink from the cup, what do you imagine you are receiving—or drinking, or doing—by that gesture?
Many do not drink from the cup at Communion. In your own words, what important aspect of the celebration are they thereby missing out on?

7. Blood is experienced as symbolic of both *life* and *death*. When we drink from the chalice, taking into ourselves the blood (the *life* of Jesus), in what sense are we also committing ourselves to his *death*?

8. In the present Roman Catholic tradition, immediately before the reception of Holy Communion we are invited to turn *to one another* and give a sign of Christ's peace. In terms of the covenant liturgy of Exodus, why might the Church have placed this *community gesture* as an immediate preparation for Holy Communion?
Does this suggest, perhaps, another dimension to those traditional words "Holy Communion" than simply a personal encounter between oneself and Jesus?
You might like to discuss the implications of this for your local community of faith and even the wider community.

CHAPTER TWO

The Vision That Drove Jesus

I will stand at my post,
I shall station myself
on my watch-tower ...[1]

There are two aspects to the story of Jesus that believers can overlook. The first is how deeply he loved his people. The second is that throughout his life, whether during the silent years of Nazareth or the tumultuous months of his public career, Jesus was constantly maturing and growing (cf. Luke 2:52). In an earlier time, our insistence on the divinity of Jesus may have clouded our capacity to appreciate the depth of humanity which he shared with us. We would have thought of him as motivated more by love for God than for his people. Nor could we tolerate that this divinely-human person struggled with the immaturities and limitations that are part and parcel of created existence. Yet the data confronts us in the Gospel writings! Sadly, theological preconceptions had blinded us to the richest dimensions of this beautiful human-divine encounter that we call Jesus.[2]

For What Did Jesus Stand?

Jesus loved his people. He was impelled by a vision of what they could become. This was a love from which he never retreated, a love that would eventually constrict his choices to Calvary. The decision to love was what cornered Jesus: he died out of love for his people.

The depth and scope of his love is most poignantly captured as he begins that final week of his life, in the moment of his glimpsing Jerusalem—the beloved and precious city. Jesus pauses, and Jesus weeps.

Many of us inherited a faith shadowed by an excessive hostility toward "the Jews" who killed Jesus. Perhaps we were overly influenced by the anti-Semitic culture of our childhood years. Or possibly, in our youthfulness, we uncritically absorbed the dark picture of "Pharisees, Sadducees, and the leaders of the people," as portrayed so aggressively in the Gospel of Matthew.[3] What we could not see with clarity was, perhaps, the deep affection in which Jesus held his nation, his own flesh and blood:

> "Jerusalem, Jerusalem, you that kill the prophets and stone those who are sent to you! How often have I longed to gather your children together, as a hen gathers her brood under her wings, and you refused!" (Luke 13:34)

The city of Jerusalem, heartland of Hebrew faith, tradition, and history, represented for Jesus all that he had dreamed and hoped for his people. This was the city of God; it contained the Temple of God's very presence. For the sake of the people he loved, he would walk into that city, staking his very life on the cleansing of the Temple courtyard, confronting those who were leading the nation to ruin. They might abandon and crucify *him*, but he would never abandon *them*. Even on the Cross he sings over the nation these final Psalms:

> "My God, my God, why have you forsaken me?"
> (Matthew 27:46, Psalm 22:1)[4]

> "Father, into your hands I commit my spirit."
> (Luke 23:46, Psalm 31:5)[5]

The startling truth is that Jesus died for his people. He did not die consciously for us, nor—in a sense—for God. He died for the nation who were his flesh and blood, who had given him the richness of their tradition and in whose faith he had been brought up. The depth and pathos of this love between Jesus and his people is captured by Luke's version of him coming to Jerusalem for that final confrontation:

> As he drew near and came in sight of the city he shed tears over it and said, "If you too had only recognized on this day the way to peace! But in fact it is hidden from your eyes!" (Luke 19:41-42)

Jesus not only loved his nation—he held for it a tender vision of peace and hope. This encounter with Jerusalem occurs in the final week of his life, a coming-to-climax (as it were) of all the pressures and energies that charged his ministry. He had long been compelled by that vision of the covenant born to the nation on Exodus. It was the clash between this covenant ideal (of what could be) and the disturbing realities being lived around him (what actually was) that finally moved Jesus into public activity. In order to grasp the fundamental meaning of baptism in our lives, let us explore what made Jesus "go public" in his own baptismal choice.

The Baptismal Decision of Jesus

Jesus was a faithful and practising Jew. With Sabbath regularity (cf. Luke 4:16), in the synagogues of his childhood, adolescence, and early manhood, Jesus would have been immersed in the stories of Exodus and the subsequent wrestling of the nation throughout its history to live that high vision. The readings of the prophets were about little else! The weekly ritual of the Word of God was a constant confrontation with the challenge to live as God's nation of justice and mercy. Incessantly, the nation's angry prophets had railed against the loss of integrity, the loss of national and personal will, that so readily showed itself in a readiness to trample on the rights of the poor. Exploitation of the weak, the voiceless, and the poor is the recurring sin of Israel's history.

The covenant commitment had been to the precise opposite: a nation protective of the marginal, a community in which all could bathe in the tender, human expression of God's loving concern. Yet, by the time Jesus reaches the age of thirty years, he sees around himself a nation deeply divided between rich and poor, the righteous and the unclean, the gifted and the sick, insiders and outcasts.

His God-given spirit of justice is deeply offended; he can no longer stay in the backwater of Nazareth, secure from the dangerous engagement:

> … then there seemed to be a fire burning in my heart,
> imprisoned in my bones. The effort to restrain it wearied me,
> I could not do it! (Jeremiah 20:9)

These fierce words of Jeremiah had been scored in the heart of Jesus over many Sabbaths; now, and probably under the sway of John the Baptist's fiery preaching, they had come back to challenge him. For John had taught Jesus to "open his ears" and "to listen like a disciple" (Isaiah 50:4)[6] to what was actually happening in the society of their time:

> … they have sold the upright for silver
> and the poor for a pair of sandals …
> they have crushed the heads of the weak into the dust,
> and thrust the rights of the oppressed to one side …
> (Amos 2:6-7)

The words might be the ancient words of Amos, but the reality was right here in their midst. Israel, in the time of Jesus, was a sharply divided nation, giving the lie to that high ideal that had inspired their ancestors in the wilderness of Sinai. The little people of Jewish society, those with no effective voice in the ordering of things, were being cast aside and rejected. "By what right do you crush my people?" Isaiah had cried, long before. Now, in his own time, Jesus was awakening to the contradiction between Sabbath proclamation and social reality: "By what right do you crush my people and grind the faces of the poor?" (Isaiah 3:15).

Like the prodigal son in his own later story, Jesus too "comes to his senses." Fired by concern for his faithless people and driven by love for his abandoned poor, he makes a momentous decision to redress the wrongs done to the cherished covenant. He will leave his home and family, step away from the social respectabilities of his current lifestyle and dedicate himself to demonstrating the richest implications of the Exodus covenant. In him, the vision of the covenant community will find living expression. The poor, the sinners, the outcast, tax collectors, prostitutes, the sick and the unstable, and all those considered ritually impure, were "bone of his bone and flesh of his flesh" (cf. Genesis 2:23). This is still society's fiercest challenge, the arena of human interaction where the call to conversion is the deepest. The elusive cultural question—"Who am I?"—cannot be seen as different from that more demanding question, "Who are we?" The genius of the gospel is to name this as, ultimately, the major human quest: to *find* our identity, not *mine.* My truest self emerges in relationship with my sisters and brothers.

This is why the stories of the Gospels are termed *sacred.* They are perennial stories, stories that configure the never-ending human search for wisdom and inner freedom; stories that remain true whatever the culture, and whatever the situation or era of history. We "find ourselves" by "finding others" in a new and reverent way. Jesus traveled this curve of learning. At the age of thirty, he "awoke" to what was happening around him. His eyes were opened and his heart enlarged. Society's treatment of those who were considered incapable of contributing to the accepted social fabric—the outsiders—finally offended him sufficiently into action. He is pushed toward decisiveness; he commits the act of baptism. He was baptized—might one say?—*toward* the sick, the oppressed, and the alienated.

To them he would speak; amongst them he would live; with them he would even eat as companion and friend. His graciousness would restore their dignity; his companionship would be covenant indeed. In him they would know the tender graciousness of the God he himself had come to experience. His lifestyle amongst the people, now so dramatically recast, would be a challenging proclamation that *this is the shape of God's covenanted community.* Like the protesting prophets of old, Jesus now declares:

> I shall stand at my post,
> I shall station myself on my watch-tower. (Habakkuk 2:1)

It is a public declaration to live henceforth in a radically new way. Being so public a stance, it is sealed by the gesture of baptism—a public, total washing of one's being. It is the commencement of a new life.

Go up on a high mountain,
messenger to Zion.
Shout as loud as you can,
messenger of Jerusalem!
Shout fearlessly,
say to the towns of Judah:
"Here is your God!" (Isaiah 40:9)

Hesed and Emet

The baptismal decision of Jesus was to live with those considered beyond the pale. The covenant, as we noted in the first chapter, is all about the formation of community, a new way of being a people. We can certainly see from this where later Christian theology of baptism would see it as the sacrament by which one entered the community. But what sort of community was it?

One could call it the community of God's love: the community *in* which—and *through* which—people would experience God's gracious ways of forgiveness, acceptance, and love. Such a community was designed to challenge the alienating and dismissive ways of society at large. In short, this community's way of being together would confront sin.

The Hebrew people spoke of their covenant with God in terms of love. But the love they imagined the covenant to be about was best described by the use of two words, *hesed* and *emet*. When they spoke of God's covenanted love, they spoke of God's *hesed* and *emet* in the one breath (Exodus 34:6). As God loved them, so would they love God. We do well to grasp the specific meaning of both these terms if we are to appreciate the commitment that drove Jesus.

Hesed
Love, in the sense of loving-kindness, mercy, tenderness or compassion. It speaks of a God whose heart is capable of being deeply moved when confronted by human suffering and need. This is a God with a "heart of flesh" (Ezekiel 36:26), who is deeply hurt by the nation's infidelities (Hosea 2). It is a love that washes feet; it speaks of a body that is *given* for you.

Emet
A word with the basic meanings of *true* and *faithful*. It is a word that expresses the constant fidelity of God's love for us, a love on which we can afford to depend. It attempts to capture the *changeless* nature of God's love; when paired with hesed, they are often translated as *faithful love*. It names the *truthfulness* of God's commitment to us, a loyalty that will never waver. It speaks of blood that is *poured out* for you.

In his own relationship with the God he called *Abba*, Jesus had himself experienced this *hesed* and *emet*. In that prayerful encounter, the energy of *hesed* and *emet* (seeded deep in his being, as in us all) was released. Jesus, born in the spirit and likeness of God, now found that spirit rising within himself. In the words of Paul, his "hidden self grew strong, through faith," and he begins that painful process of maturation-in-life that would be completed only on Calvary.[7] His life amongst "the crowds who followed him" would bathe them graciously in that same *hesed* and *emet*. His would be a love that could be trusted, a reverence that "justified" those whom it touched—allowing them to experience (as had he) a relationship with God that was worth trusting with one's life. They, in their turn, having been graciously dealt with, are now capable of being *just as gracious* to others—and community is born.

The language of theology will call this effect "redemption" or "salvation": but the human reality spoken of is simplicity itself. Jesus lived to the full the covenant described in the book of

Exodus. He did not take away the Commandments, he lived them in their fullest dimension. An uncomplicated person himself, Jesus reduced the Decalogue to a single "commandment" to love one another, even at the cost of our lives. This, for Jesus, was how one *passed over* into God, how *communion* with God was achieved: in a community of *hesed* and *emet*. For Jesus, as for Moses in that original liturgy of Exodus 24, communion with God and communion with one another were the same reality.

Baptism and Community

The Gospels were put into writing decades after the death of Jesus. They do not attempt to be day-by-day accounts of what happened in his life. We approach them more faithfully by seeing them as a set of stories and memories about Jesus, but stories and memories that were shaped and presented to address the contemporary concerns of those church communities for which they were written. The Gospels can sometimes appear as complex documents, but they manage to tell us much about the beliefs held by early communities of Christians concerning Jesus. They give us an authentic and trustworthy portrait of his character and person.

In Mark's Gospel, the earliest, we encounter Jesus making several significant journeys outside Israel and into the territories of the surrounding, non-Jewish people. On one such journey, a Syro-Phoenician woman challenges Jesus to broaden his boundaries beyond his own people, amongst whom he believed his mission lay (Mark 7:24-30).

The meeting with the Gerasene demoniac (Mark 5) is another encounter with people of non-Jewish, even pagan culture. Significantly, in this story, the cured demoniac—now "in his full senses" (verse 15)—himself becomes a missionary for the *hesed* and *emet* he had so graciously received from Jesus.

It is also in pagan territory, near Caesarea Philippi, that Peter is emboldened to declare his belief in Jesus as the Christ (Mark 8:27-30). The Roman settlement of Caesarea Philippi lies well beyond Israel's border, and this important declaration by Peter forms the turning point of Mark's whole Gospel presentation.

These stories indicate that within the very Gospel stories themselves we have clear evidence that the mission of Jesus was considered as inclusive of non-Jewish cultures. Here we can trace the dawning realization that the horizons of the strictly national covenant we first met in Exodus were being reconsidered and even redrawn.

Initially, within his own Jewish culture, the covenant was seen by Jesus as inclusive of all—even "sinners and outcasts." The Gospel stories seem to stretch this boundary further, to non-Jewish participants. We know, of course, that in Paul's life as a missionary, this broader inclusivity becomes a serious contention with the Jerusalem church.[8]

What then are some implications of this for the Eucharist today?

Inclusiveness, or participation, is the defining vision of the renewed liturgy since Vatican II. The clarity we gain from the Gospels of the inclusive mind of Jesus exerts pressure on the language we use in liturgy, on the embrace and shape of the rituals we employ when worshipping, and on that delicate interplay of consciousness between the mentality of the congregation and those who lead it as ministers.

Inclusiveness in liturgy has much to do with the physical setting of any celebration—with back seats and front seats and the spaces (physical and mental) between participants. Inclusiveness has much to say about what we *imagine* is going on in the Eucharistic Prayer: On whose behalf does the priest utter the prayer? Over what (and whom) are the words of consecration spoken? Whose life is being offered to God as "a living sacrifice of praise"?

Inclusiveness challenges what the bread we use for Eucharist looks like; the dramatic range of gestures and responses; and our capacity to devise workable ways for all present to drink meaningfully—that is, *drink*—from the cup.

Inclusiveness is about the style and format of music employed and its capacity to gather people into the mystery of their ennoblement in Christ.

Inclusiveness is about who are deemed welcome to attend the ritual of the Eucharist and who are not.[9] In short, inclusiveness is a gospel mindset. It is covenant in action.

In the wider world of our day, is not inclusiveness one of the driving realities confronting all nations and cultures in ways never experienced before? In his own culture and time, the boundaries of inclusivity with which Jesus had to cope were capable of stretching his imagination and energy. But consider the vastly expanded platform of today's global concerns: issues of international debt, the tyranny of north over south, the enslavement of poorer economies, the exploitation of the underpaid workforces in emerging nations, militarism, homelessness on a scale beyond imagining, racism, the medically deprived, the unwanted remnants of human history and colonization. Somewhere—in all of this global pain—communities who believe in Jesus, and the covenant of human relationships for which he lived and died, have their crucial role to play—even if only as signs of hope. Desperately needed are communities of *hesed* and *emet*: embodiments of God's gracious tenderness and acceptance.

We are coming to realize that this is precisely what baptism is about: for faith-filled people in a world of injustice—as was the world of Jesus—to commit themselves to the same vision that filled him. It is a deliberate choice to enter this sort of community (an earlier theology would have called this *being saved*). The sentiments of the adult baptismal candidate are no different from those of Jesus, the Lord:

> I shall stand at my post,
> I shall station myself on my watch-tower. (Habakkuk 2:1)

In the Gospels, the word most commonly employed for "sin" is *hamartia*, a Greek term from archery meaning "to miss the target," or perhaps "to miss the point."[10] It can thus be said that the baptismal decision to enter a community focused into *hesed* and *emet* will *take away* our *missing the point*. To enter this sort of community is to be "on target" or "saved," and to be filled with a graciousness that sanctifies.

When we gather on a Sunday to celebrate the Eucharist, in a real sense it is our baptism that we are celebrating and furthering. The *martia* (or point of it all) is Christ. One way the early Greeks used the term *baptizo* was in relation to the trade of cloth dying. To change the color of a garment it was placed into the boiling dye. To see whether the color had yet "taken," the cloth had to be lifted out, inspected, then dipped again into the mixture. The word the Greeks used for *repeatedly dipping into the dye* was *baptizo.*

On each Sunday of our lives, therefore, believers gather to "dip themselves again into the mixture—or the story—of Christ," and we do so repeatedly throughout our lives "until the color takes." It is a lifelong process.

But let us be clear about one thing: we gather not merely to hear the stories of how Jesus lived; we gather to be immersed *in the story,* and the community living *hesed* and *emet* is the Story. The graciousness of Jesus either happens or does not, depending on how we actually come together, on how we *are* with one another when we do come together. All worship, all sacraments, and especially the Sunday eucharistic celebration, are defined by the quality of our presence to one another—are we *hesed* and *emet* for one another as we gather?

A whole dimension to Sunday liturgy lies in this: What is the manner of our gathering and with what human warmth do we welcome? Until we begin to shift Catholic consciousness toward what it means for us all *to gather in Christ,* then opening greetings like "We gather today … " will remain a contradiction to the human experience of those present.

This loss of the human dimension to gathering is one constant observation that younger people, or strangers who drop by on a Sunday, seem to be making. This hospitality of the Eucharist is something we ignore to our peril: those who arrive in isolation and who are allowed to remain in isolation during the ritual are indicative of a lapse of covenant on the part of the community. Communities might not be able to stand shoulder-to-shoulder, but the eye-to-eye welcome at the door as we gather for worship is not beyond us. Eye-to-eye is well on the way toward heart-to-heart …

Eucharistic ministers, especially, might find this ministry of welcoming a significant extension of their usual role. If, later in the ritual, they are to offer participants the Body and Blood of Jesus, why not actually assume this hospitality prior to the liturgy? As ministers of the Eucharist are they not equivalently saying, "On behalf of the Church I offer you the presence of Christ"?

Yet even beyond ministers, is not hospitality a "ministry" common to all who gather? Might not a parish distinguish itself by the quality of its welcome: no one enters our celebration unnoticed, unwelcomed, unwanted. In such an understanding, the Sign of Peace commences well prior to the Gathering Song and is extended into the ritual. Giving to one another what is the essence of the peace of Christ becomes a community's mission and way of life.

Other practical issues might flow from this appreciation that a *new* covenant lies at the heart of our Sunday gatherings. The first liturgical choice made by all who attend is the choice of where to be seated. To sit in the same place, amongst the same people, and to give the Sign of Peace to those same people every week seems a trivialization of the gesture. Where we choose to sit and with whom we thus align ourselves (to say nothing of any spaces thus created between participants) is the first sacramental choice upon arrival. The singing, the participation, and the experience of a vibrant community can often be determined in those first conscious moments upon entering the "familiar" church.

Covenant is about *hesed* and *emet*, consciously shouldered. It is about opting into the process of making New Covenant as Jesus did. It is about inclusivity and the truthfulness with which we all can say, "My Body is given for you; my Life is poured out for you." When these realizations begin to come home to us all, then perhaps even the music we use will prove no great problem and our communities will sing as never before. Our struggle to be singing communities might evaporate to the degree we have something to sing about:

> Go up on a high mountain,
> messenger to Zion.
> Shout as loud as you can,
> messenger of Jerusalem!
> Shout fearlessly,
> say to the towns of Judah:
> "Here is your God!" (Isaiah 40:9)

For Discussion

1. What richness do the words *hesed* and *emet* (the two aspects of God's love) add to your commitment to live the faith? Why are both terms so important? In your experience of the community of faith in which you live, where do you suggest the community is challenged by the realism of these words?

2. The Church asks that all baptisms now be done in the public domain, in front of the whole Church community. From our reading of the life of Jesus, what is your understanding of why the Church insists that baptism be public?

3. In baptism, it is not the water that baptizes a person: only the story of Jesus can wash a person into God. The washing with water is the *sign* of our commitment to entering the Story.

   When we take to ourselves the story of Jesus' life and are baptized, several things are said to happen:

   - we become children of God,
   - our sin is "taken away,"
   - the gates of paradise are open to us,
   - we enter upon what the Gospel writers called *eternal life*.

   Keeping in mind the baptismal story of Jesus, and the meanings of *hesed* and *emet*, what deeper understandings can you now see to the meanings of these religious phrases?

4. Jesus was a person who loved with a passion and clarity of the original Sinai covenant. His love was a love that "saved" others into believing that they too were capable of *hesed* and *emet*—and thus of "saving" others. We remember Jesus for this. We call him the savior of us all.
   Speaking in terms like this, and staying close to the Gospel stories of Jesus' life, what do you see as the mission and task of the Church in today's world and times?
   For what purpose does one join the Church?

5. In Greek, one meaning of *baptizo* is *to be overwhelmed.* This is one reason why, in the early Church, candidates for baptism were fully immersed in the water: it was a way of symbolizing the impact of the story of Jesus.
   A second meaning (from the dye-makers of Greece) was to be *repeatedly dipped* into the solution (until the color held fast). In this sense, one's baptism is never fully completed in one's lifetime: one is constantly growing into the fullness of the mystery of Jesus.
   Given these two basic meanings to the important word "baptism," how would you respond to the question: "Why go to Mass every Sunday?"

6. The hospitality of God's covenanted community begins as people arrive at the door. Welcoming is our first covenant gesture. In this view, everyone present is a minister of eucharistic presence.
   You may like to discuss this matter of hospitality—especially with reference to your own community and its possibilities.

7. The gathering of the community—issues such as where we sit and with whom we sit—can be of great importance to the life of the coming celebration.
   You may like to share your comments on this, especially with reference to the possibilities within your own community.

8. When the covenant is embodied in the world, God is worshipped. The first task of any Christian community is to become a community that lives the gospel vision of Jesus: the *new* covenant.

   If the celebration of the Eucharist is no longer available to a local community (say, through the absence or lack of a priest), what elements of the ritual—above all else—should be the focus of that community's gathering?

In such a situation of priestly absence on Sunday—and this may become more common—what do you believe is the individual's primary responsibility: to find another Mass somewhere else, or to support your local community in a liturgy of the Word?

CHAPTER THREE

A Ritual of Compassion

Take your bread and
feed God's hungry,
open wide your
welcome door![1]

In Mark's Gospel, the eucharistic teaching is not restricted to the account of the Last Supper. We shall see later that when he tells the story of the Last Supper, Mark arranges his material to make an unexpected—and potent—point about the Eucharist, but his major insight is contained in the twinned stories of feeding the people: the *first* miracle of the loaves (Mark 6:30-44) and the *second* miracle of the loaves (8:1-10). Why should Mark have gone to the trouble of including two?

Firstly, let us be clear that by the time Mark came to write this Gospel (sometime between the years 65-70), there was really no need for him to recall to his community exactly what Jesus did at the Last Supper.[2] True, there would be *some* value in preserving intact a summary of Jesus' actions on that important night, but by and large everyone in the community for which Mark wrote would have been well aware of what Jesus actually did *for they had been doing it, just as Jesus had, every Sunday since!* Being immersed in the ritual of the Eucharist on a regular basis, there was little need for Mark to inform the Christians of his day as to what that ritual originally looked like—the performance of the ritual would itself ensure it was never forgotten. But what seems to have really concerned Mark was that by the time of the late sixties (thirty years after Jesus had died), the Church for which he was writing, frightened by the crisis upon them,[3] was in real danger of forgetting *the meaning* of the rituals they celebrated every Sunday. In these two stories of the Feedings, Mark astutely confronts them with what the rituals of bread and wine actually *meant.*

But why the *two* stories?

Both stories are similar. All the elements of the first story are involved in the second. The elements, however, are slightly rearranged in the second: some things spoken by the apostles in the first are put into the mouth of Jesus in the second; five loaves and two fish (seven objects) become simply seven loaves in the second; in the second story, fish are mentioned separately, almost as an after-thought; the first makes a point of the people sitting down in squares of hundreds and fifties—a clear reference (for a congregation with some Jewish background) to an incident in the Exodus;[4] twelve baskets of remainders in the first become seven in the second; similarly, five thousand participants become four thousand; and—most importantly—the *setting* of the story differs. Yet these stories occur only (what we call) a chapter apart from each other.[5]

The setting of each story differs. The first occurs in a Jewish context, the second in an environment that is pagan, non-Jewish.[6] Whatever was the original mind of Mark, one can see method in balancing the stories so deliberately: the eucharistic vision of Jesus for his own beloved people (the covenant vision) is now extended right out into the lives of pagans (the church of this particular Gospel was probably Roman). Mark is pushing the horizons of the Jewish covenant into a more universal vision for humanity.

Feeding the Five Thousand

Let us concentrate on Mark's *first* story, the Feeding of the Five Thousand (Mark 6:30-44). What precise insight about the meaning of the Last Supper is Mark here making? Be quite sure that this is a eucharistic story and not one simply "proving that Jesus was God and could do miracles" (as many of us would have learned in our childhood).

The context in which the story is placed is important. Jesus, awaking to the enormity of the task before him, sends out the twelve apostles in his name, two by two, into all the villages of Galilee (Mark 6:7). They return to Jesus, full of all that had happened (6:30). Being human, they need to retreat to a quiet place to recover (6:31). Jesus suggests they cross the lake by boat into the less settled country on the far side. But the crowds would give him no rest—they follow on foot around the bottom of the lake and arrive before the boat carrying Jesus and the Twelve. On arrival, Jesus is faced by a crowd "like sheep without a shepherd," so "he set himself to teach them at some length" (6:34). The artistry of Mark is superb, for the whole of the coming story is already contained in these telling phrases. Jesus is already living up to what would be his Last Supper words over the bread, "This is my body, take it," and over the wine, "This is my blood poured out for you."

Jesus, although exhausted by previous commitments, had given everything he had to those desperate people: he summoned resources within himself that were way beyond expectations. He gives totally: *hesed* and *emet* demand no less.

But now the apostles approach Jesus. Although tired themselves, they still have the compassion to notice the crowd's plight as evening falls. The people are hungry, and it is no place to spend the night. As happens in many of the Gospel stories, the apostles ask *Jesus* to do even more for the people. And Jesus, having just "nourished them" with everything he had, turns on his Twelve and simply says: "Give them something to eat *yourselves*" (6:37).

The apostles, startled by the enormity of the challenge and very conscious of what it might cost them, reply: "Are *we* to go and spend two hundred denarii on bread *for them* to eat?" (6:37).

They frame a *sensible* question. But captured here is the perennial quandary of humanity in terms of the poor and disadvantaged. Is there any question—even in the world of our own time—more dangerous than what the Twelve have just asked? They have voiced the fear within the hearts of us all: Are *we* to take responsibility for *them*? This one fierce question continues to search us today—a piercing gospel challenge to our social, political, and international zones of comfort and relationships. To face this apparently simple question with honesty will demand a conversion of life that is both personal and national:

- In a world of 56 million homeless, by what yardstick do we measure any one nation's immigration policies?

- In a world in which poorer countries are crippled under burdens of international debt and unfair trading policies, how do we rate the apostles' question?
- In a society so economically driven that the well-off become so at the expense of the health, well-being, and education of the voiceless, the immigrant, the elderly, or the young—what disturbance in our hearts (and churches) is caused by the apostles' probing question?
- In societies riven by ethnic outrage or declaring themselves not responsible for the dispossession of indigenous peoples in the past, is this not still the uncomfortable gospel question?

One could obviously go on at length with such applications. This Marcan story clearly sees such down-to-earth issues as the very stuff of the Eucharist. In this view, the Eucharist is no mere Sunday ritual for "worshipping God," no simple act of prayer. For Mark sees, underneath the all too familiar rituals of the Eucharist—and perhaps masked by those very rituals—disturbing connections to the real world of human flesh and blood. The Eucharist is ultimately about human life and death. Yet for so many of our contemporaries, the eucharistic celebration appears irrelevant, so unconnected to real life. Such perceptions must force those of us who continue to celebrate the Eucharist into a serious re-evaluation of our rituals.

In the story, the apostles rise to the occasion and offer the crowd everything they possess by way of food. Like Jesus, they themselves now choose to live up to those Last Supper words: "given for you, poured out for you." Many Gospel stories concern themselves with this ennobling transference of consciousness from Jesus to others. As the story opens, Jesus gives everything he has to the hungry, demanding crowd. Now the Twelve are compelled to do no less.

Witness the artistry of Mark. As we shall see, the point he wishes to make concerns the meaning of the eucharistic ritual (celebrated in his community each Sunday). Mark now slices the developing story with an alarming eucharistic reference. Into this apparently everyday event of a hungry crowd late in the day, Mark inserts a piece of the easily recognizable Sunday ritual. The words he carefully chooses would have shocked his listeners into the connection he wishes to make with the Last Supper:

> Then he *took* the five loaves ... raised his eyes to heaven and *said the blessing;* then he *broke* the loaves and began *handing them* to his disciples to distribute among the people. (Mark 6:41)

There are *four verbs* in this eucharistic formula. These same four verbs still occur today in whichever Eucharistic Prayer is used in any Sunday celebration. They are words engraved on the memories of our people:

> Then he *took* ...
> *said the blessing* ...
> *broke* the loaves
> and began *handing* them
> to his disciples to *distribute* ...

In the New Testament, the Last Supper accounts differ slightly in their precise wording. Luke and Paul include the phrase: "Do this in remembrance of me," which is not found in the Gospels of Mark and Matthew.[7] This additional phrase, when used by Paul and Luke, obviously refers to the gesture Jesus has just done with the bread (and wine). Jesus is saying: "from now on carry out this ritual as a way of remembering me," that is, keep doing this gesture as your life-giving ritual. Let us note, however, that the gesture involves four verbs, *four distinct actions:*

- we *take* "our bread" (or our time, our talents, our possessions, our lives);
- we take such gifts *appreciatively* (we "raise our eyes to heaven," and thank, or bless, God for them);
- we then *break* the gifts (our time, our talents, our possessions, our lives);
- we hand the gifts to others—*give* them—that they in turn might enjoy a life fully human.

Startlingly, in Mark's feeding story, these four verbs take on a new dimension of meaning. Although Mark does not make use of the command, "Do this in remembrance of me," there is a truthfulness in which we can say that—in this Feeding Story—Mark is urging his church to *do* these *four verbs* with their lives (just as the apostles were urged by Jesus). And further, that when his church in Rome *acts according to these four verbs*, when they *live with utter generosity*, it is the life of Jesus that they are *doing*—indeed, they are *being* Jesus.

This is simply to say that what we do describes who we are. We enter a holy communion with God by committing ourselves to live like Jesus. The Church's own Eucharistic Prayer plays upon the exact same theme by inviting God to look upon *us* (our community's attempt at living *hesed* and *emet*) and to see *him* (God's own child, Jesus) in us:

> Look with favor *on your Church's offering* (i.e. us),
> and *see the Victim* (i.e. Jesus)
> whose death has reconciled us to yourself.[8]

This seems to be the point of the story of the Feeding. In a real sense, this is not so much a miracle done by Jesus, as a miracle done by the apostles: it was *their bread and fish* that was donated (their evening meal). And Jesus, after saying the prayers of gratitude, gave their food *back to them* for its distribution. Jesus was standing back from the action, letting them assume their rightful dignity in the supplying and handing over of the gifts; "Give them something to eat *yourselves*," he had said (Mark 6:37).

The structure of the remainder of the story bears out this emphasis on the apostles as the major players in the event. Twelve apostles donated their resources to the hungry crowd. When all is said and done, they collect twelve baskets of leftovers: one for each apostle. The point of the story is clear: when you give with total generosity, you receive back more than you ever gave; that giving is a way of receiving; that feeding others is a way of being fed; that a life given in service is a life discovered; that to serve is to care for one's own selfhood.

We will see that this pattern of giving and receiving—this movement of handing out and then receiving back—forms the very framework of the Church's ritual of the Eucharist.

The Framework of the Eucharist

When we look at the major elements that form the liturgy of the Eucharist, we begin to realize just how significant is the story of the Feeding. Unfortunately, even the admirable renewal of Vatican II has not capitalized on the beautiful symmetry of involvement that this miracle story reveals: that in giving, we receive; that in feeding, we are fed.[9]

The early Church incorporated this fine insight directly into the structure of the ritual, building the Eucharist around an involvement of all participants in these two major events: the *procession of gifts* and the *procession for communion*. It is almost as if this meticulously structured story of the Feeding furnished the pattern for the shape they gave to the Eucharist. These two reciprocal processions were preceded by a proclamation of the life of Jesus from the Gospels:

We *listen* ...
We *respond* with generosity ...
We are nourished by so doing.

There arose, therefore, a three-fold pattern to the flow and expression of what we came to know as the Eucharist:

1. The Word of God is proclaimed in the assembly. Jesus, the embodiment of God's Word, who lived the *hesed* and *emet* of God in a loyal covenant amongst even outcasts and sinners, is proclaimed in the Gospel memories as the image and vision of what this attentive community could become.
2. In a second movement, there is a physical procession of "all who have heard the Word," and all who have prepared for this act of worship by dipping into their larders and possessions at home, carrying them to the celebration.[10] This *response of generosity to*

the Word is the community's way of saying: "Yes! We will obey what we have just heard! As Jesus lived the covenant, so shall we!"

3. Some bread and wine from this procession is then prayed over by the presiding bishop "*in memory of Jesus.*" The gifts of this generous community become the presence of Christ (in a later Church language, they become "consecrated," and having been thus rendered sacred can in turn render sacred *those who consume them*). Here, in a third movement, this same community now comes forward a second time, but on this occasion with their own hands outstretched to receive a taste of that same bread and wine: to be nourished on the Body and Blood of Christ.

   It is the story of the Feeding of the Five Thousand in ritual form: to the degree we give, to that degree are we fed. What we firstly give is *physical sustenance* to the poor who surround us; what we receive in return is a *sustenance for our spirits*, an inner nourishment that is signified by the taking of what looks like "food and drink" into our bodies. The whole gesture indicates that the "food and drink" given in the spirit of Jesus become the continuation of his person in our lives. In that precise sense we "receive" him.

To use more colloquial language: we hear in the readings the story of how Jesus lived—we will obey that story, live it, take it "to heart." And to construct this new community that Jesus lived and died for, we dig into our substance and come forward with "gifts for the sustenance of others." The gifts are ourselves—they represent our own lives. Like the Twelve in the Feeding story, it is *we* who are *given for you*, it is ourselves who are poured out *for you*.

The Eucharistic Prayer then captures the joyful quality of such self-donation: we remember (and sometimes even sing) how Jesus died living this vision, and how he saw that same consciousness as possible in us. Then, returning in a second procession to seal and express that communion, we "swallow the Story," consume the person portrayed in the Gospels, and "take inside ourselves" the Blood of this *new* (and never-ending) covenant for humanity.

Notice that the whole edifice is supported and grounded in the Word of God, which is clearly heard and deliberately obeyed. This would seem to suggest three observations:

- As a Church we would do well to work more intensely on the quality of the Word's presentation. The readings must impact on the consciousness of the assembly if they are to inform the remainder of the celebration. Remember the pattern of Exodus 24: without obedience to the heard Word, there is no Communion.
- When, for reasons beyond a community's control, the Sunday celebration of the Eucharist is unavailable, clearly the least that should take its place is a vital presentation—and appropriation—of the Word of God (the readings, especially the Gospel). The whole point of Christian worship is to become a *Gospel community*. This is what living the new covenant means.
- If, in such non-clerical situations, the Church encourages a lay-led celebration of the Word of God, then one might ask (in light of the Exodus pattern) how we can rightfully deny such a community the remainder of the sacrament (which the Word informs)? How might we begin to think about worship in the absence of a priest when we realize that it is the *Word of God* that creates and ultimately shapes the Christian community?

The Procession of Gifts

In Catholic churches today, the procession of gifts (once known as the Offertory) is performed by a small group of people. It can sometimes be seen as merely a way of preparing the table for the celebration. Basically, bread and wine are carried forward, but frequently also the collection money and possibly candles. What are we trying to demonstrate with this ritual, especially in light of the story of the Feeding of the Five Thousand?

Originally, this was an action that involved *everyone* in the assembly. Our understanding of what happened in the early Church is that far more than bread and wine were carried forward to the presiding bishop: what the community "carried forward" were gifts for the sustenance of the poor of the community.[11] Even in our limited knowledge of what actually went on in those faraway years, we do know that the faithful carried to their bishop a variety of gifts for the support of the poor: bread and wine (staple foods), oil and wax (for warmth), blankets, flowers, and clothes. St. Justin, a widely traveled educator from the second century, wrote of this collection of gifts:

> Those who are well off, and who are also willing, give as each chooses. What is gathered is given to him who presides to assist orphans and widows, those whom illness or any other cause has deprived of resources, prisoners, immigrants, and, in a word, all who are in need.[12]

The procession would approach the bishop singing—this was a joyful sharing of what they had. One early piece of Scripture sung as an accompaniment to this procession seems to have been, "God loves a cheerful giver"! The bishop stood, deacons at either hand, to accept the gifts of offering. He passed them to the deacons who carried them for storage in the small transepts built into the basic shape of the Roman basilica (or public meeting hall). These varied gifts were destined for distribution during the coming week.[13] At the conclusion of this procession, the bishop would wash his hands (the origin of a gesture we now have no real need for keeping).[14]

The bishop would then invite the deacons to bring back to the table (not called an altar until later in history) sufficient *bread and wine* to give *all in the assembly* a small taste.

Only the elements of bread and wine were chosen from amongst the range of gifts, for bread and wine immediately summon up the memory of Jesus on the night before he died. Only "bread and wine" will trigger this connection. They are a potent link to the substance and culture of Jesus. Taken from the wealth of gifts destined for the poor, "bread and wine" were placed on the table in the center of the community.

The bishop then sang the prayers that explicitly recalled the memories of Jesus at the Last Supper. The great song of the Church is its Sunday Eucharistic Prayer. It was led by the singing presider, but the community joined in with a regular acclamation; everyone participated in the connection being made between *their gifts for the poor* and the gift of *the life of Jesus* to his nation—as he died for love of his people, so would this community "die" (through generosity and service). Hence the *Three Great Acclamations* that now punctuate every Eucharistic Prayer, celebrating the community's consciousness of being the presence of Jesus today:

1. **The Sanctus**

   Holy, holy, holy Lord, God of power and might,
   Heaven and earth are full of your glory,
   Hosanna in the highest.
   Blessed is he who comes in the name of the Lord.
   Hosanna in the highest.[15]

2. **The Consecration Acclamation**

   Christ has died!
   Christ is risen! [Us!]
   Christ will come again ... [16]

3. **The Doxology**

   Through him, *with* him, *in* him,
   in the unity of the Holy Spirit,
   all glory and honor is yours, almighty Father,
   for ever and ever.[17]

Once the Eucharistic Prayer had commenced, the bishop sang over the tabled bread and wine one specific prayer of great importance in the tradition: it is called the Prayer of Epiclesis,[18] and it occurs in some form—and with the same gesture of the priest's outstretched hands over the gifts—within every Eucharistic Prayer. It is the prayer of *calling down the Spirit of God* upon the gifts of bread and wine so that they be changed into the Body and Blood of Jesus.

In this prayer our thinking about what happens in the Eucharist is revealed.[19] The clearest tradition of the Church (whether in East or West) is that the *consecration of the gifts* is a way of ensuring the *consecration of the community* (who consume them). The second part of our current Roman Epiclesis Prayer (after the Consecration) makes this very clear:

Grant that *we*, who are nourished by his body and blood [the gifts], *may be filled* with his Holy Spirit [the Epiclesis Prayer over us], and become *one body, one spirit* in Christ.[20]

Remember that in the early Church the small amounts of bread and wine now on the table in front of the bishop are but a token of all the gifts of the community that had been stored for distribution during the week (the clothing, the oils, the wax, and so on). And when, before the Consecration, the bishop extended his hands over the bread and wine and prayed, "And so, Father, we bring you *these gifts*. We ask you to make *them* holy by the power of your Spirit ... "[21] —over what range and collection of gifts was the bishop truly praying? In other words, of what bulk of generous offerings are the tabled bread and wine representative? We need to see the connection between:

- the small amount of *bread and wine* on the table,
- the *bulk of offerings* stored in the transepts, and
- the *community embodied* by those gifts.

The secret of the whole ritual, of course, is that all three are one and the same! To consecrate one is to consecrate all three—they cannot be divided. One's gift is oneself. The person I am is revealed in what I do. When it all comes down to basics, the gifts that are consecrated on the table to become "the body and blood of Jesus" *contain* the very people whose gifts they are. The gifts *symbolize* the people; they *express* the people's generosity in following Christ.[22] Or, in the Latin imagery of the early Church, the gifts are a sacrament of the Body of Christ. The bread is not his Body (not in the mere physical sense) but a sacrament of his Body. The wine is not his Blood (again, not in the mere physical sense) but a sacrament of his Blood (the covenant). To consecrate the gifts of bread and wine is to consecrate the assembled community: it is the community—and its gifts of bread and wine—that become the fullest extension of the Real Presence of Jesus.

This is poetic language of the highest order. It is the community's generosity and gracious care for others that brings it into the Spirit of Jesus. As in the Exodus covenant, no one in this community will be in want: all will be treated with divine dignity and love. The poetic language of the Sunday ritual tries to capture this ennoblement in the prayer immediately after the Consecration in Eucharistic Prayer II:

> we offer you, Father,
> this *life-giving bread*,
> this *saving cup*.

The *life-giving bread* is a poetic expression for the community's generosity: it is *our* bread that gives life to others. At the same time (and at a deeper level of meaning), the bread is a poetic symbol that describes Jesus. What we offer God is *Jesus*, and yet Jesus is the name *we* are ...

The *saving cup* is a poetic expression for the community's commitment to the covenant vision of a new, compassionate humanity—a world in which no person will be treated unjustly. We drink that cup of commitment. Only such a *cup of blood* offers hope to a struggling world: it alone can "save." It is also truly a *cup of blood* in that a generosity such as the assembled gifts imply will cost us: it may even be, as it was for Jesus, the death of us. His consciousness is *ours*, his calling and vision are ours, and our appreciation of this ennoblement of our lives is captured in that same prayer that continues:

> We *thank you* for *counting us worthy*
> to *stand* in your presence and *serve you*.

The Communion Procession

The procession for receiving Communion is the second time the assembly approaches the table. This procession balances and completes the first procession with gifts. Each sheds light on the meaning of the other. Both are needed for eucharistic understanding and participation.[23] Notice how the interplay between these two processions in the early Church's Eucharist was faithful to the structure we found in the Feeding Story of the Gospel: *to the degree we give generously, to that degree we are fed just as generously:*

THE TWO PROCESSIONS

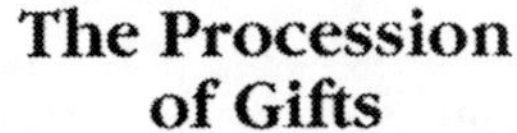

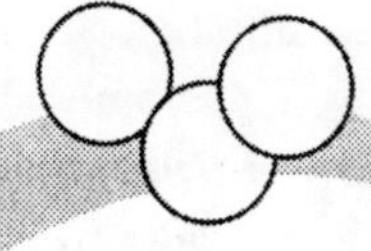

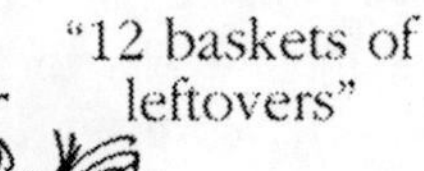

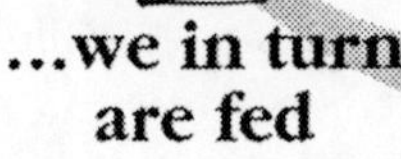

The Communion ritual commences with the community donning the mind of Christ as he " dares to pray" his own prayer to *Abba*.[24] When we pray, Christ prays over the whole of creation. On us has been conferred the honor of stepping into the standpoint and person of Jesus. We assume his consciousness. We are offered a part in his mission.

The Sign of Peace then becomes an embodiment of all that the new covenant envisions. One hopes it is no mere nod to the same circle of acquaintances every Sunday, but an opportunity for us to move out to the stranger, to the timid, to the hesitant. It is the *peace of Christ* that we offer and embody, not just "peace" in general. It calls for a dignified and conscious exchange, expressive of the Mystery that binds us to one another. Situated immediately prior to the Communion procession, it becomes the first step (as it were) into recognizing *the holiness of true communion* we are about to dramatize in the reception of bread and wine. In our tradition, the Sign of Peace now plays an integral part in the reception of the Eucharist.[25] Sadly, church furnishings can often limit the scope and impact of this important ritual of community participation. Happily, the Communion Procession is not hampered by furniture. It is a bodily movement of the whole congregation in a statement of who they are: one people, one Body, committed to the one covenant named Jesus.

From the startling symbolism of using one loaf of bread, St. Paul argues strongly that all participants thereby form the one Body of Christ (1 Corinthians 10:17). We have yet to satisfactorily address the issue of the type of bread we customarily use in the Eucharist, but even when making use of pre-cut hosts, the Church is adamant that all the bread to be distributed at Communion should have been previously "brought to the table" in the Procession of Gifts—and not be supplemented by breads from the tabernacle.[26] In this, the Church is insisting on *the intimate connection between the two processions:* as we give in the Spirit of Christ, so are we fed by that same Spirit. This image of giving and thereby receiving (taken from the Feeding stories of the Gospels) adds beauty and poignancy to the gesture of coming with hands cupped and outstretched to receive the Bread of Life in return for "the bread" (amongst other things) that we have ourselves provided in our gifts for the poor—our hands are outstretched to receive what the outstretched hands have given.[27]

The minister holds the bread before us and focuses our understanding with the challenge: "The Body of Christ." It is a phrase that totally summarizes the new covenant. In this context, the minister is equivalently saying to us: "You are offered the new community of God's *hesed* and *emet*, as it was lived in Jesus." Then, like the Hebrews at Sinai when challenged by Moses with the details of the covenant commitment, we too reply together: "Amen!"—"We are this people! We will obey!"

Notice an important movement from "*I* eat the bread" to "*We* will obey": the interplay between personal gesture and communal consciousness. I watch *you* eat the bread and commit yourself to this covenant community; you watch *me* eat the bread and commit myself to that same covenant and community. In the gesture, feeding off the same story that is Jesus, our relationship to one another changes forever: we live together in Christ. Holy Communion is no private affair.

It is the same with the cup of the covenant, but with an added dimension that comes with the expression, "The Blood of Christ." Just as in Exodus, where the commitment to live the covenant as a nation was sealed by the sprinkling of blood over the people, so now is this new covenant sealed by each of us "taking the Blood of Christ" into our hearts. This is a sprinkling of the inner person, of our hearts and spirits. It denotes inner submission and conversion.

But more as well ...

There is a dimension of suffering to the word "blood" that is not present in the term "bread." Drinking the Blood of Christ commits a person to the sufferings of Jesus, the "pouring out of his life for many" in selfless *hesed* and *emet*. We are confronted with the realism that all loving involves a cost, just as it did for Jesus. What we are offered when the minister holds before us the eucharistic wine is nothing less than the cup of the sufferings of Christ today. I watch *you* drink from it; in turn, you watch me drink: a gesture that binds me to you and you to me. The gesture of the common cup commits me to live *with you* today's dangerous covenant of love for humanity, whatever the cost may be of living that Real Presence of Christ. It is communion with God, but just as clearly a Holy Communion with one another, one that we enter and "receive" together.

Each Sunday, then, we gather to symbolize our identity in Christ. We gather to *build the holy community* and to keep alive the vision that impelled Jesus. What he achieved in his short, redemptive life is now being completed by ourselves. On us has been conferred his consciousness and mission: we are his contemporary presence. This is the mystery[28] of our faith so wondrous that we cannot refrain from proclaiming it in song:

> When *we* eat this bread and drink this cup,
> *we proclaim your death*, Lord Jesus,
> until you come in glory.

For Discussion

1. How has your understanding of the story of the Feeding of the Five Thousand been deepened or challenged?
   What would you now see as the actual point of the story?

2. It has been said that the Church's Eucharist is built on two great processions: the presentation of our gifts being one, the reception of God's gifts in return being the other. These two major experiences in the Sunday liturgy once involved all present.
   How well do you feel our Sunday ritual captures this understanding?
   How conscious are most Catholics of this dynamic relationship within the Eucharist of *giving* and then *receiving*?
   Are our congregations conscious of the relationship between the collection of monies for the poor and the bringing of bread and wine in procession to the table?

3. In the Eucharistic Prayer each Sunday, what really is it that we *consecrate*: the gifts of bread and wine alone, or the community

whose gifts they are? In the Church's mind—as evidenced by her prayers before and after the Consecration—what is the full story of what is going on? Do bread and wine alone become the person of Jesus, or does the community (symbolized by the bread and wine) become that person as well?
What is your experience of this? And what parts of the Church's own prayer—either before or after the Consecration—do you find best express what you believe?

4. Drinking from the cup of the Lord's blood is to drink from the sufferings of the Lord today. What might this mean for a contemporary community of believers?

5. The balance evident in the early Church's *two-procession structure* (involving all participants) has been largely lost in current Sunday practice. To lose the intimate connection between the Procession of Gifts and the Communion Procession, is to risk losing the meaning of the whole liturgy. One sure way to re-educate our churches in the meaning of Eucharist is to *let the ritual educate.*
Discuss what this might mean in your own situation and community.

6. If one's baptism is a commitment to form with our immediate faith companions a gospel community that embodies the way Jesus lived, then our *Sunday obligation* to *attend Mass* is a commitment to one's local community of believers. Should the Mass—for whatever reason—not be available, then the Sunday *commitment to the community* surely stands.
In light of the Gospel stories and the liturgy of the covenant at Exodus, what is your reading of this obligation? And what conversion of attitude is needed amongst us if we are to honor it to the full?

7. It has been said that since Vatican II, the primary issue of the Eucharist is not whether—or how—*Jesus* might be present, but

whether *we* are truly present: indeed, that to the extent *we* are more fully present, so is he.
Discuss the challenges and implications of this.

8. "Lord, look upon this sacrifice which you have given to your Church; and by your Holy Spirit, gather all who share this one bread and one cup into the one body of Christ, *a living sacrifice of praise.*" (Eucharistic Prayer IV)
Why "living sacrifice"? And, "of praise"? About what reality is the Church trying to speak?

CHAPTER FOUR

That Final Meal

To be on earth
the heart of God [1]

The Jesus we meet in the Gospels is not a complicated person. He was born into a Hebrew tradition that he apparently lived to the fullest. The core of that tradition was the covenant made at Sinai as they left Egypt. The God who had proved loyal to them would be honored by a corresponding loyalty on their part: Hebrew social life—the Ten Commandments—would embody God's mercy and tenderness.

In his baptism, Jesus committed himself to that ennobling vision. He would live the tenderness of God amongst those very people who were feeling its absence so deeply. The startling element in his lifestyle was that he even *ate* with them, inviting himself into their companionship. It was the manner of this gracious companionship that so changed his disciples. Burning with true justice for those lost, hungry crowds, Jesus would give nothing less than everything—even if it cost him his life. He saw himself as *given for* them, and in living faithfully that conviction, came to know the full dimensions of what it meant to live in God. In this lay his unique self-sacrifice a loving service to his people that would end on the Cross. For Jesus, to *pass over into God* was no mere Sabbath ideal but rather the down-to-earth realism of a life dangerously focused by faith in the covenant. To be attentive to this demanding conjunction of life and faith is the task for us all—indeed, the point of all religion. It implies an attentive posture before life, a posture that the tradition calls obedience.[2] For Jesus, this obedient engagement with life's reality came to a poetic climax on that evening when he gathered for one final meal with his friends.

This meal, which anchors the total faith perspective of Jewish participants, is a complex blend of poetry, story, ritual, and symbol. For contemporary readers like ourselves, the Last Supper ritual is even more intricate: its rituals of bread and wine actually take their meaning from *two distinct stories* in the book of Exodus:

1. **The Story of the Covenant of Sinai (Exodus 24)**
   We studied this story in chapter one. It involves the reading of the Law by Moses, their commitment to it as a nation, and the subsequent sprinkling with blood to symbolize their "passing over" into communion with God. The story climaxes in a ritual of *communion* and its symbolism centered on *blood*.

2. **The Story of the Night They Left Egypt (Exodus 12)**
   This story precedes the story of the covenant liturgy. It portrays the eating of both the unleavened bread and the flesh of the slaughtered lamb (their people's homes were marked with its blood). God's avenging angel "passes over" blood-marked homes as the people prepared to begin on that night their arduous journey toward a promised future. The focus is on *journey*. This story's symbolism centers on *unleavened bread*.

Both stories are important:

1. Exodus 24 asks: How do we come into true *communion* with God?
2. Exodus 12 asks: What will nourish and sustain us on this demanding journey of life, the *journey* into God?

Both stories are attempts to address the one human question: *How to pass over into God's life?* This is the primary concern of all faith. There is, in a sense, no other question. Our Jewish ancestors knew it as the recurring question of life, the perennial issue that each generation and era must face. Indeed, their religion was built on stories of the past (like the Exodus), but the question addressed by their forbears in that long distant time was still the question with which they were wrestling in their own time.

We have to understand that in the Hebrew mind, past stories described current realities: the journey into God—or into compassion, into love—had to be completed afresh in *every* epoch, had to be integrated into their being at every stage of their history. Exodus and Passover were thus *never* completed, *never* finalized: the nation was *always* "on exodus," *always* in the process of "passing over" into God. Their stories of how this was accomplished "long ago" were thus called *sacred* or *eternal*: they outlined the enduring human condition. They remain true in all ages, valid for all cultures, applicable in all circumstances. The Hebrews preserved such important stories within the framework of their religious rituals—making the truths of a past wisdom accessible to people in the present.

HEBREW RITUAL THINKING I

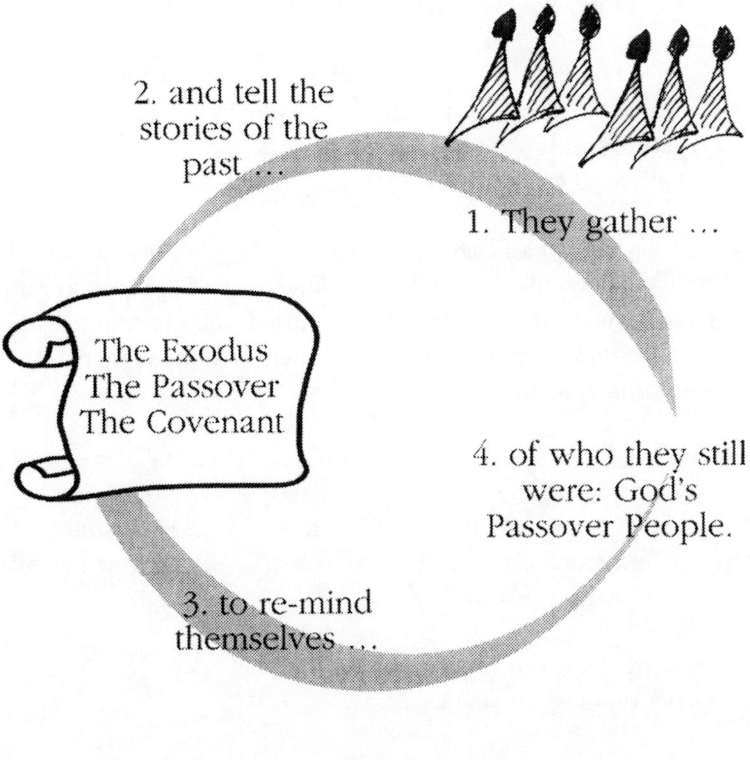

1. They gather ...

2. and tell the stories of the past ...

The Exodus
The Passover
The Covenant

3. to re-mind themselves ...

4. of who they still were: God's Passover People.

Giving Bread and Washing Feet

On this important evening of his life, Jesus gathered with his few remaining friends to celebrate the Passover and thus immerse them in that ancient memory that alone could provide meaning and energy to their existence. In the rituals of food, drink, and song they would recreate the Passover with its old and treasured meanings for life: they would dramatize that ancestral event so as to nourish themselves with its perspectives of truth and commitment.

Jesus had celebrated this ritual each year of his life. He and his disciples were well familiar with the spread of meanings associated with the unleavened bread of Passover:

- As Passover coincides with the commencement of Spring, it celebrates life's recurring beginnings. Unleavened bread, not contaminated by the left-over leaven of the past year, expressed that aspect of newness and fresh perspective:

  > This month must be the first of all the months for you, the first month of your year ... For seven days you must eat *unleavened bread.* On the first day you must *clean the leaven out of your houses* ... (Exodus 12:1, 15)

- The Passover feast commemorates the night of their departure from Egypt on the great trek toward the Land of Promise, toward their God and the covenant of Sinai. Their food for the journey was the flesh of the slain lamb, eaten with bitter herbs and *unleavened bread:*

  > You must keep the feast of *Unleavened Bread* because it was on that same day that I brought your armies out of Egypt ... This is how you must eat it: *with a belt round your waist, your sandals on your feet, and your staff in your hand.* (Exodus 12:17, 11)

- To share the *unleavened bread* was to build oneself into the solidarity of the community of Israel:

> anyone ... who eats leavened bread will be outlawed from the community of Israel. (Exodus 12:19)

On this important night of his life—and steeped in such a tradition—Jesus sensed these rich dimensions of unleavened bread and their application to the ordeal which lay before him:

- new beginnings,
- sustenance on the journey,
- solidarity together.

This would be the last Passover Jesus would ever enjoy in the company of these loyal disciples whom he loved—a realization that sharpened his perceptions. He also knew well the forces aligned against him—several of his close friends were themselves Pharisees and the opposition from officialdom was hardly covert. If this was to be his "going-away song," then Jesus would use the whole range and depth of poetry contained in the rituals of Passover to summarize his perceptions and to convey his final testament to these faithful few.

At the expected time, Jesus *took* the unleavened bread into his hands. He saw it as representative of everything for which he had lived—this unleavened bread, awash with covenant associations, was his whole life. On this final night, profoundly moved by the mystery that was his life, he *thanked* God for it. Deliberately, he *broke* it—as indeed he had tirelessly "broken" his life amongst the crowds. He then *gave* it to those who were there—again, just as he had "given his life" for his people, time and time again.

He asked his disciples to take it and eat it: to take inside themselves (in the manner of food) his whole way of living. Keep in mind the associations carried by this unleavened bread on the night of leaving Egypt: it signaled a new beginning; it was food for their life's journey; it was a statement of solidarity as one people.

These Exodus associations would have filled the minds of his disciples as he gave them this "unleavened bread of Passover." But Jesus then shocks them by adding to those traditional words this most unexpected rider: "This is my body, given for you."

In Hebrew thought, the body is the person. The term "body" is not a reference to what we would call the physical dimensions of the person—skin and bones—it is a way of speaking about the total personhood. Equivalently, Jesus is saying: *this is me, this is who I am, this is how I have lived.* Eat me. Eat my way of living. Take me within yourselves and feed your minds and hearts on my lifestyle.[3]

Jesus is summarizing his total life: he was "given" to others, he lived "at the service" of others. He saw himself "like bread," in that people fed off him, were nourished by listening to him, by paying attention to him. To be "like bread for the taking" was to enter that frame of mind which Jesus called the covenant, a commitment to love and to be "for others" at any cost.

When his disciples accepted from him the piece of bread—which Jesus had now named as "his life"—they were making a decision in relation to the life that they had seen him living all those months. They would now eat—not simply the unleavened bread of Exodus—but the new dimensions of how Jesus had himself lived that Exodus mystery while with them. Taking and eating the bread, they were "receiving Jesus." Not physically so. The bread was a symbol carrying something far richer: his whole person, character, and approach to life. Eating the bread is a way of declaring openly one's total acceptance of the life and mind of Jesus—his life alone can nourish our inner being. To hold out my hands to "receive the bread" expresses that it is all gift, that I am one who comes needy, and that, like my hands, my whole being is open.

Add all of this to the rich memories the disciples already carried about unleavened bread at Passover and the fullness of this supper gesture becomes apparent. The gesture of taking within oneself (i.e. eating) the way Jesus lived the covenant (his body, his person) becomes a demonstration of three convictions:

1. like the unleavened bread of Exodus, it marks a *new beginning* in one's life,
2. like the unleavened bread of Exodus, it is the *only food* to sustain life's journey, and
3. like the unleavened bread of Exodus, it binds all who eat into a *solidarity as one people.*

Jesus takes that ancient ritual of unleavened bread and repaints it with meanings taken from his covenanted life. He had lived the Passover journey of loving fidelity to the covenant; within a day he would be prepared to die for it. His life fully embodied what these complex rituals of bread and wine had expressed symbolically all those years—Jesus' lived faith is bread for a full life (Exodus 12)—to then commit ourselves "to obey" that story is to drink the blood of the covenant (Exodus 24). For Jewish people, this is the all pervasive tradition of their faith and the fire in their hearts. But during this supper, Jesus *becomes* the tradition, his life a more compelling expression of the tradition than the tradition itself! Hence the startling words: "Do this in remembrance of me" (Luke 22:19).[4]

There are two distinct meanings to this short command. It can be read correctly as a command to "do this ritual" in the future as one that recalls "me" (Jesus) to mind (and will no longer be a recollection of the Exodus from Egypt). But it may just as correctly be read as a command to "do in your lives what this ritual indicates," to go forth and live what the ritual symbolizes: go out and *do it*. Both meanings are permissible: the ritual we dramatize must be consistent with the lives we are leading—for otherwise the ritual becomes a lie. This is the strength of the ritual of Passover as Jesus did it that night: in Jesus' simple ritual of gratefully taking bread, breaking it, and giving it to them, the disciples recognized the consistency of it all with his way of living. This is the point of human rituals: a kiss must be an expression of love; a word must reflect the inner heart of a person; a gesture must be sincere—otherwise we (and society) are destroyed in the process of dishonesty.[5] This consistency of life and ritual is the constant challenge for worshippers:

> If you are bringing your offering to the altar and there remember that your brother has something against you, leave your offering there before the altar, go and be reconciled with your brother first, and then come back and present your offering. (Matthew 5:23)

The early Church inherited from Jesus these Last Supper rituals of bread and wine. They performed them every week in his memory. The rituals contained rich nourishment for life when those involved appreciated fully the Hebrew origins and Exodus allusions of bread and wine. But by the time the Gospels were put to writing, many church communities were no longer Jewish in culture, so the rituals ran the risk of becoming *insincere*[6] and their connection with real life becoming clouded. When this intimate connection is lost, the temptation within all religious systems is to develop a system of rituals and language so "religious" as to be beyond the grasp of ordinary believers. Worship can then become esoteric, of "another world," overly sacrosanct in character, mysterious and specialized, with a life—and clientele—of its own. When rituals begin to lose their obvious meanings for life, they can be seen as irrelevant and their hold on people's lives is lessened. All rituals are subject to this process and perhaps something like this was already occurring by the time the Gospels came to be written down. For the authors of the Gospels, while reporting the basic facts of the rituals used by Jesus, inject into their narrative dramatic connections to real human living that could not be misread nor easily misunderstood. This is surely the supreme artistry of those who arranged the Gospel stories.

John's Eucharistic Teaching

The highly poetic language of John's Gospel can obscure the graphically down-to-earth nature of his view of the Eucharist. John's account of the Last Supper makes no mention of bread and wine. In this Gospel, the language of bread and wine is found elsewhere.[7] Instead, when telling of the Last Supper, John has Jesus perform an action, not with food but with a basin and towel. This does not alter in the slightest the depiction of his character: the spirit and person of Jesus that emerges is just as striking. With the water, he washes the feet of his disciples, wiping them with the towel. And as in the other Gospels, John carefully aligns his Last Supper account to the Jewish Passover traditions:

> Before the festival of the Passover, Jesus, knowing that his hour had come to pass from this world to the Father, having

loved those who were his in the world, loved them to the end. (John 13:1)

The washing of feet is given a Passover meaning—the context makes this plain. But John simplifies the four-fold gesture with bread and wine (taking, thanking, breaking, giving) into this single gesture of gracious hospitality—the bathing of feet.[8] In the culture of the day, it was a welcome into the home and life of the one performing the washing (usually, of course, done by the home-owner's servant). This socially acceptable gesture of community (you are welcome in our home) becomes for Jesus a profound offering of intimacy and communion. As Peter tries to resist the moment, Jesus says: "If I do not wash you, you can have no share with me" (John 13:8). This is a Semitic expression meaning he can have "nothing in common" with Jesus.[9]

For John, this gesture of loving welcome is the meaning of the Eucharist: in John's mind, the gesture with "bread" is described by the gesture of foot washing. The outcome, a commitment to building the loving community, is the same. In other words, the vision of the Ten Commandments is fulfilled in people whose mindset—like Jesus—is gracious hospitality. It is the mindset of Jesus that is here presented: this is how Jesus lived the covenant. In this brilliant portrayal of Jesus at the Supper, John bridges the gap between Jewish traditions and surrounding cultures, but bridges them by depicting a gesture familiar to non-Jews (foot washing) that is at the same time faithful to the meanings behind the rituals of Judaism (unleavened bread and covenant blood).

For Jewish people, bread breaking and wine sharing (the common table) symbolized our communion with God through communion with one another. The uniqueness of Jesus is that he extended that tradition of covenant living beyond the boundaries of one nation. John's account of the Last Supper catches that outward broadening—yet the symbolism is still the same: a genuine hospitality toward one another (deliberate community) expresses our communion with Jesus. Unless our worshipping communities portray such evident hospitality, we run the real risk of having "nothing in common" with Jesus. There is simply no other way "to pass over into God."

The core comment that interprets the washing of the feet is what Jesus speaks to Peter (John 13:8, quoted above) about having a life "in common with" him. This is a communion statement. Yet a language for Holy Communion, far more familiar to Catholics, occurs in chapter six of John's Gospel. There John has Jesus speak frequently of "eating his flesh" and "drinking his blood" (John 6:53-58). These are graphic images, easily mistaken when read out of context of the debate occurring in that chapter between Jesus and "the Jews."[10]

Catholics, introduced to such terms as "flesh" and "blood" when young, can read them almost literally and as if the Gospel is supporting a virtually physical presence of Jesus in the bread and wine. This is certainly not what John means. The argument between Jesus and his opponents on this occasion is about whether Jesus represents the true and only way into God; as John would poetically express it, is Jesus truly "the bread of life"?

In this engagement, "the Jews" cannot accept this, precisely because they know his human background, "his father and mother"—"Surely this is Jesus son of Joseph," they object (John 6:42). In John's portrayal, Jesus counters this argument by resorting to unusually graphic language:

> If you do not eat *the flesh* of the Son of man
> and drink *his* blood,
> you have no life in you ...
> For *my flesh* is real food
> and *my* blood is real drink. (John 6:53-55)

The words are emphasizing precisely what "the Jews" were not able to accept: that the human, incarnated life of Jesus, with its everyday struggle in fidelity (his "flesh and blood"), is the only way into true life in God. Unless we "eat" that flesh, "drink" that blood, we cannot have life in ourselves. John's use of the terms "flesh" and "blood" expresses his insistence on the *earthiness of faith* and the incarnated reality of Jesus. His is an appeal to immerse ourselves, and to seek God, in the ordinariness of our lives—in those Nazareth, family, and social realities that religion can sometimes be seen to avoid.

Our constant Catholic tradition describes the presence of Jesus in the bread and wine as "real." Precisely what is to be understood by this word has proved a challenge just as constant.[11] Too many people think of this "real presence" of Jesus as if he were there as he was when he walked the streets of Israel. In the Church's mind, *such* a *physical* presence is not intended. In any sacrament it is the *risen* Lord who is present and the key understanding is that he is present there *sacramentally*. "Sacrament" is the word we must probe if we are to render the ritual of the Eucharist relevant and compelling to the people of today.[12]

Nor is this struggle over the meaning of the word *sacramental* a recent concern. In his *Summa Theologiae*, St. Thomas Aquinas teaches that Jesus' body is not present in the sacrament of the Eucharist "as in a place" *(sicut in loco)*.[13] Aquinas stresses that while Jesus' presence is *real*, it is not a physical presence in the commonly understood sense.

One thing we can surely say is this: when celebrating the Eucharist together, Christ is so rendered present as to be *truly*, *really* and *substantially* experienced. Indeed, his presence has such realism that it is totally involving of our own lives and provides a context for life so meaningful that it can only be described as "through him, with him, and in him." One would not call such a presence *physical*, but it is well described as *real*.[14] His total reality—and ours—is contained in the bread and wine. One could say that all those realities that constitute the person of Jesus are—in the Eucharistic celebration—*earthed* amongst us forever. When I am in the presence of the Eucharist, I am immersed in everything that I have come to know by the name of Jesus. This is nothing less than a living engagement with the person of Jesus.

John emphasizes these "flesh and blood" aspects of our faith. In his Gospel, these words will assume deeply poignant realism in the bloody, bodily conflict of Calvary. John's is an earthy faith. The Jews misread his use of the words "flesh and blood" as something literal: "How can this man give us his flesh to eat?" they are quoted as saying (John 6:52). Unfortunately, some popular Catholic understandings of flesh and blood have been closer to how these opponents took the words (i.e. literally) than to what John intended by them (i.e. as symbolic).[15]

Mark's Eucharistic Insight

We have studied Mark's story of the Feeding of the Five Thousand (6:30-44) and referred there to the parallel story of the same event amongst non-Jewish people (8:1-10). These two stories form the basis of Mark's teaching on the Eucharist, but he nevertheless presents the Last Supper (14:22-25) in a context designed to convey far more than a simple report as to "what Jesus did" at the meal.

Scholars have unlocked in Mark's Gospel a writing technique not unique to that author but certainly used to great effect by him. It is called the technique of framing. We read the Gospel in divisions called chapters, but such divisions of the text were unknown to the original writers. Mark organizes his writing by employing frames to highlight passages of particular importance. Let us look at the specific frame he places around his account of the Last Supper.

We use the term "frame" to mean what it normally means to us: a careful structure placed around something of great value to protect its meaning (or to indicate its meaning more clearly). Like a framed print, the attention of the reader is meant to be focused toward *the contents* of the frame and not to become too distracted by the makeup of the frame itself. In chapter 14 of the Gospel we find the Last Supper account framed by two stories written in parallel, two stories of betrayal:

Frame A: The Treachery of Judas

While at table, Jesus declares that one of them will betray him. Distressed, they *all* protest their innocence. Jesus declares again that one of them is untrustworthy.

Teaching: The Institution of the Eucharist

Jesus *takes* the bread, *thanks* God for it, *breaks* it, and gives it to them: "Take it ... this is my body [who I am]." He then takes the cup, speaks the blessing, and they all drink from it: "This is my blood, *the blood of the covenant, poured out for many*."

Frame B: The Treachery of Peter

As they leave, Jesus declares they will all lose faith. Peter asserts that he alone (of all of them) will not. Jesus predicts that Peter will deny him. But Peter more earnestly declares: "If I have *to die* with you, I will never disown you." Mark adds: "And they *all* said the same."

The construction of this frame is very powerful. Using bread and wine, Jesus commits himself to the covenant—like the bread he was "given for" others, and his commitment to live the loyalty of God's justice is trustworthy. The essence of the Eucharist is the commitment: I am given *for you*; my blood (if necessary) is poured out *for you*. Like the God who brought the Hebrews out of Egypt, Jesus' word can be trusted.

It is contrasted firstly with Judas, secondly with Peter. In both frames, all the Twelve assert their preparedness to stand by Jesus, even (in Peter's case) to die for him. The contrast with "blood poured out for you" and Peter's shallow words could not be greater. Mark is challenging us to see the words of Jesus at the Last Supper as a commitment to stand in solidarity and loyalty *with one another*, no matter the price. To do the eucharistic gestures and to speak the eucharistic words is primarily a public commitment to stand with one another in a new covenanted way—and the words must be trustworthy. Only in the seriousness of that mutual commitment to one another is Jesus truly present amongst us. Otherwise, like Judas, the Twelve, and especially Peter, our words are hollow.

What Body and Whose Blood?

When our communities now gather for the Eucharist, what do we imagine is going on when the priest speaks the words Jesus spoke at the Last Supper (the words of Consecration)? In whose place is the priest standing as he speaks those crucial words over bread, then over wine? Is the priest simply representing Jesus, so that when the priest speaks those words—"This is my body ... This is the cup of my blood"—it is Jesus again speaking them in front of us? Are we, as a congregation, merely watching Jesus offering himself again—through the priest—to the Father as he once did on that night of the supper? Or are we *involved*? Do we *participate*?

The whole urgency of the renewal of liturgy undertaken by Vatican II was for the congregation to participate in what was happening. What the council meant by that was more than finding ways for some of the congregation to read, for others to distribute the Eucharist, to be ushers, musicians, or commentators. The vision of the council was that the *whole congregation* would come to *participate* in the crucial meaning of what the Eucharist is really all about. The congregation—all who are assembled—are intimately involved in what is occurring at the Consecration: so it is our gesture, not simply the gesture of Jesus.

It becomes clear then how the priest who presides is speaking on behalf of all who are present and gathered.[16] When the presider speaks, it is the voice and speaking of the whole assembly. These spoken words over the bread and wine are the words of the people over the bread and wine: the people who have been baptized into the mind and consciousness of Christ.

> These are *our* words:
> This is *my* body which will be given up *for you.*
> This is the cup of *my* blood …
> It will be shed *for you* and *for all* …

Several important issues must be addressed here. In the Eucharist it is *our* body that is given, *our* blood that will be poured out. In his memory we offer *ourselves* as we become *part of* what he did and who he is. Today, there is no one else to offer to God if not ourselves: for Jesus of Nazareth is not here on Sunday, we are. He made his offering once and for all. Our privilege is to now make *our own offering*, made in the same spirit, the same generosity, using the very same words over the very same symbols of bread and wine. The Eucharist is about *ourselves* and not, in a sense, about Jesus. We dare to make the offering *through him, with him and in him*, but the person offered today is ourselves. God has invested us with the reality of Jesus; this is our ennoblement and our calling.

Grasping this, in the realism of the words used and challenged by the Gospel accounts we have examined, we must ask the question: *To whom are we speaking these words of Jesus?* In our mind's eye, toward whom are we looking as we say, "My body is given for you"? To whose lives are we committing ourselves as we dare to say, "My blood will be shed for you and for all"? To whom is the congregation speaking? With whom is the assembly "making covenant"? What is the point of it all? With what immense mystery are we here involved?

Unfortunately, as we have inherited the ritual today, these crucial words of commitment remain beyond the reach of the assembled people and are reserved to the priest. This is how things are. Currently, the people are invited to participate via the sung Acclamation immediately following the words of Consecration (which we will study later). However, one can appreciate that the loss of participation in these key words of Jesus can lead to a shallow grasp of what is actually going on and (at times) to a total misunderstanding of the Eucharist. We must slowly recover the challenging loyalty—the spoken commitment—captured by Mark's framing of the Last Supper story.

It was a commitment St. Paul saw as lying at the heart of Eucharist. We have analyzed some Gospel passages of the Last Supper, but even before they were written, Paul makes mention of the supper ritual in his first letter to the Corinthian church (11:17-34).[17] His concern is precisely their lack of solidarity and mutual commitment: the rich and the poor were attending but not then sharing a full companionship in the meal that followed. So he declares their ritual empty:

> I hear that when you all come together in your assembly, there are *separate factions* among you ... So, when you meet together, *it is not the Lord's Supper that you eat*; for when the eating begins, each one of you has his own supper first, and there is one going hungry while another is getting

drunk ... have you such disregard for God's assembly that you can put to shame those who have nothing? (1 Corinthians 11:18-22)

For Paul, the validity of the Eucharist turns on a commitment that is mutual, serious, and carried through into life together. Like the Hebrews at Sinai, the way into communion with God is through communion with one another. God's presence amongst us will never be realized until we recover this dangerous sense that Holy Communion cannot exist solely between myself and God: religion is no private affair. Rather, Holy Communion is the name we give to that loving reality between human beings that we call community, or covenant, or the presence of Jesus. The bread and wine are its sacrament, but the reality is deliberate community.

For Discussion

1. It is *our* living that we celebrate in liturgy: the ritual is a process by which we clothe ourselves and our current experience in the never-ending story of how Jesus *passed-over* into God.
   Discuss what this means for us. Has there been a change in your understanding of what Christian liturgy is *about*?

2. At the Last Supper, Jesus *took bread*. He named it to be his person (Hebrew: "my body"). He names that "body" as *given for others*. The Church teaches that the presence of Jesus is "most real" in the Eucharist—that is, when bread is taken gratefully, broken, and distributed for the life of others.
   What do Catholics mean by *the real presence* of Christ? Has your understanding of this mystery changed?
   When, in Communion, we *receive the real presence* of Christ, what commitment is involved in such a gesture?

3. John speaks graphically when he writes:

   If you do not *eat the flesh* of the Son of man
   and *drink his blood*,
   you have no *life* in you. (John 6:53)

   What point is John trying to make by using such unusually physical terms? What levels of rich meaning do you now see within the words?

4. John speaks of *flesh* and *blood* in chapter 6, but when portraying the Last Supper in chapter 13, he speaks only about *the washing of feet* (a gesture of hospitality). What connection do you see between these two chapters and these two unusual sets of words? What insight is John trying to convey about the meaning of Holy Communion?

5. When we instruct those making their First Communion that they will be "receiving Jesus," or perhaps, "receiving the Body of Christ," what down-to-earth reality do these religiously coded words actually reflect?

6. At the Consecration, the priest speaks the words of Jesus over bread and wine: "This is my body … This is the cup of my blood." How do all the people in the congregation participate in the meaning of this sacred moment and gesture?

7. In Mark's Gospel, the Last Supper story is carefully framed by two stories of betrayal (Judas and Peter). What particular light does such a careful arrangement place on the meaning of Eucharist and Holy Communion?
   What broadening of Catholic horizons is Mark inviting us into by this careful arrangement of his Last Supper story?

8. Pope John Paul II has expressed the hope that, as the Millennium is upon us, the Church might rise to the challenge of developing *a spirituality of global dimensions.* When we

gather as the community of Jesus for Eucharist on Sunday, what global dimensions are involved?

How would you *now* respond to the question: *Why go to Mass on Sunday?* What has changed for you in how you speak about this?

CHAPTER FIVE

Forming the Eucharistic Mind

In the shadow of God's glory we will stand[1]

The worship tradition inherited by the Church is Hebrew in origin. Later European alterations to that basic inheritance must be carefully monitored lest in the process we lose touch with some crucial ingredients of the tradition that nourished Jesus. Not that we must return to the rituals of an older culture, but we must ensure that current rituals carry into contemporary generations the *meanings* and *insights* conveyed in earlier times. Ritual does this well when its meaning is transparent and its performance is involving of participants. Otherwise ritual becomes irrelevant. One further danger is to name as traditional those rituals which do not fully deserve the name and whose origins are not as ancient as we might have imagined. Some "traditional" rituals of the Mass made their appearance during the Middle Ages and were generated in that era by a spirituality foreign to the Gospels.[2]

The very word "eucharist" is instructive in this regard. It is a Greek term translating the Hebrew word *berakah*. Unless we recover the living richness of *berakah*, so familiar to Jesus and the early Church, we will never grasp the dimensions of meaning that lie under our increasingly popular use of the name Eucharist.

In Hebrew culture there are three distinct meanings to *berakah*. It means either to praise, to thank, or to bless (the meanings are quite interchangeable when used). In some ways, *berakah* captures the foundations of all Hebrew faith in God: an abiding sense of appreciation and gratitude. God had given so much to them, done so much for them, stood by them so consistently, that the only possible response was *Berakah*!—we praise you, we thank you, we bless you for all that you have done for us! Without this profound grasp of God's goodness, no loving response is possible. In the realization of all that God had initiated in their regard, the Hebrew people developed a spirituality based on gratitude, appreciation, and joyful praise. The truly pious Jew was encouraged to exclaim *Berakah*! one hundred times each day—not as a fiction, but in a deliberate attempt to notice life's goodness and to acknowledge God as the source of it all. Such an approach to spirituality implies a constant deepening and broadening of one's sense of appreciation; it involves a desire to notice with increasing clarity those aspects of life and creation that are beautiful, good, and true. It is a spirituality that humanizes; an approach to living that flowers into graciousness and wisdom. This is a focus for faith we would do well to recover.

Jesus was educated in such a frame of mind: *berakah* pervades the 150 Psalms that formed his treasury of prayer. We read of him even publicly breaking into *berakah* song, overwhelmed by his experience of God (Matthew 11:25-27). On another occasion, he happily trades *berakah* calls with an unknown woman who praises his mother (Luke 11:27-28). And knowing how *berakah* piety was designed to develop the capacity to notice life's blessed moments (even the most subtle), we surely observe the fruits of such a practice in Jesus' life when he noted the generosity of the impoverished widow in the Temple (Mark 12:41-44), or when he delighted in the innocence of little children (Mark 10:13-16). The abiding sense of maturing appreciation (contained in the word *berakah*) is nowhere more startlingly portrayed than in the differing accounts of both the Last Supper and the Feeding stories of the Gospels.

In all these portrayals, Jesus "takes the bread" (or the loaves, the fish, the cup of wine), and "raising his eyes to heaven," he gives thanks (or "says the blessing").

On the occasions when crowds are waiting to be fed and the resources for doing so are minimal—just a few loaves and two fish—Jesus expresses his gratitude for having even that. His is an expression of profound gratitude even when what "earth has given and human hands have made" seem inadequate for the task.

However, when Jesus takes bread at the Last Supper and names it as "my body," the bread is representative of his own being, his own life and person, of how he had lived: it is for this gift (symbolized by bread) that Jesus praises and thanks God. There is a profound significance to the realism of this moment in his life.

- He is conscious of having achieved so little—even his supposedly loyal followers will lose confidence in him. From where he now stands, it is all in the hands of his God: *Berakah!*
- His own beloved nation to whom he committed himself totally (even recklessly?) has already dismissed him as insignificant. They will mock him on the Cross by twisting his very own words. In the face of that apparent failure: *Berakah!*
- In the full flow of his energy and contribution he is "cut off from the land of the living" (Isaiah 53:8), unable to carry forward or complete his life's work. For the little that his life had been, he speaks: *Berakah!*
- Taking the cup of wine, now seen by Jesus in the realism of his blood (soon to be shed), he has the courage to speak over what was coming: *Berakah!*

Jesus had grown into such an appreciation of God's goodness and loyalty that he himself would now measure up to that same graciousness—no matter the cost. His *berakah* prayer was the source of faithful commitment; no circumstance could change the things in his life for which he was so grateful. Indeed, the Passover story of his nation's Exodus from Egypt was a story of graciousness and commitment on the part of God. On this very night, in which Jesus stood most in need of inner reassurance and courage, the Hebrew rituals of Passover confronted him with the life-giving memories of the nation's past experiences with Yahweh. Grounded in those past memories of God's utter fidelity, Jesus (in this dark and deathly passage of life) had only one word of response: *Berakah!* Unless we grasp this inner dynamic of praise, thanks, and blessing, we will never come to the core meaning of the ritual that a Greek world would call *Eucharist*.[6]

Hebrew Ritual Thinking

At the Last Supper, Jesus needed to tap into a story that would move him forward into his sufferings with a love and a graciousness deeper than he had ever known. He found that story in the ancient rituals of the Passover meal. In doing those rituals (from the past), he anointed his situation (of the present) with meanings sufficient to allow him to enter the unpredictability (of whatever was to come). This poetic conjunction of the past, the present, and the future was the core of Hebrew ritual mentality. For them there was only the one story. What had happened in their sacred past was still going on in the present and would remain the only story to generate life into the future. It had been their consistent experience (hence, tradition) that only in the arena of life's struggle and suffering (sometimes named as wilderness) did the nation learn with increasing sureness the extent of God's loyalty and commitment to them. This is the Hebrew insight that only within the *challenges* of life do we humans uncover the divine dimensions of compassion, forgiveness, love, and joy that lie in the depths of our hearts. It is in this sense of discovering the riches within that we "meet the God" in whose image and likeness we are all constructed. How understandable it then becomes that their *specific* and *sacred story* was centered on the years of wandering in the desert (Exodus) and the painfulness of becoming what they would rather not be: one merciful people (Passover).

In the Hebrew tradition of liturgy, therefore, when gathering for ritual, the process involved could be presented like this:

HEBREW RITUAL THINKING II

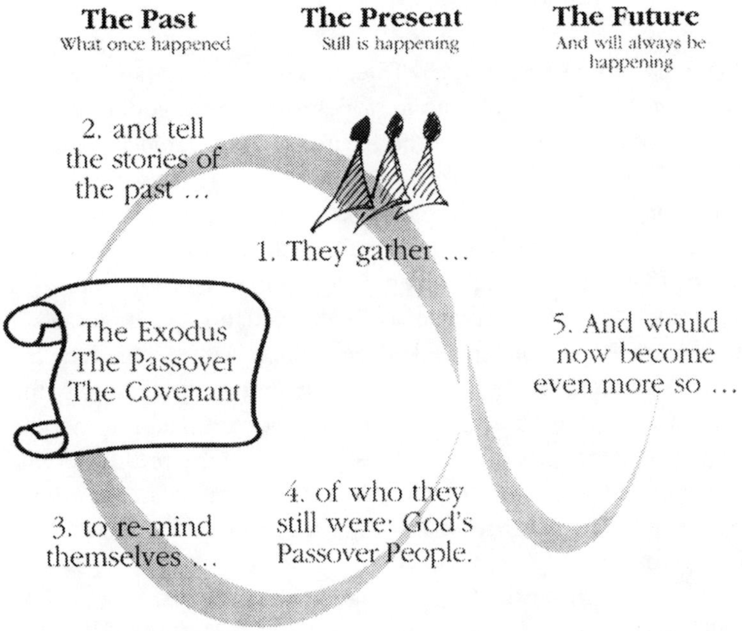

The Past
What once happened

The Present
Still is happening

The Future
And will always be happening

1. They gather …

2. and tell the stories of the past …

The Exodus
The Passover
The Covenant

3. to re-mind themselves …

4. of who they still were: God's Passover People.

5. And would now become even more so …

Note the interplay of time, of tense: what *was*, still is, and always *will be*. The Passover into God is never finished, but is rather the *always-to-be-completed story*. This was the whole point of Hebrew ritual: to take them back into past memories of the encounter with God to thereby strengthen the mind and heart of the people as they faced life's current challenges. The Hebrew tradition recognized that in past stories lay the patterns for today's life-giving response. Their rituals thus expressed the heart and soul of what had been passed down from generation to generation; rituals enshrined that tradition. Only by participating in the rituals did one learn those precious traditions and patterns for living.

The Greek culture provides us with a particularly rich word to describe such stories that carried a culture's *meanings for life* (such as Passover carried for the Hebrews): they referred to them as *myths*. The Greek term *mythos* (myth) meant "that which gives meaning and sense to life." Sadly, our popular appreciation of the word "myth" is almost precisely the opposite (something *unreal*, fictitious, *not to be believed*). True, to give meaning and sense to life, some cultures did fabricate stories about gods, goddesses, and pre-historic heroes. But not the Hebrews! Their genius was to see within historical events (like Exodus), and in the lives of the great ancestors (such as Moses), patterns of courageous response that were crucial for every generation. Of such real events and people they *made myth* by crafting epic stories that described the ideal patterns of faithful response to God. Such myths, expressed in stable rituals of worship, linked generation with generation, and provided that crucial sense of continuity and national identity that becomes the life-blood of any people. For the Hebrew people, regular involvement in such rituals guaranteed the preservation of those life-giving attitudes of mind and heart that the rituals expressed. The purpose of healthy rituals is to carry forward the best of the past.

It is this vital sense of the linkage between the *past*, the *present*, and the *future* that Christian faith inherited from Hebrew life and which became the framework of the Eucharist. We will never renew Catholic ritual unless we appreciate in a fresh and deliberate way this interplay between what *was*, what *is*, and what *will be*. Nowhere is it more artistically expressed than in our Eucharistic Prayers—yet, sadly, its subtlety may elude us. The core of eucharistic renewal in these times is for congregations to relearn the lost art of ritual thinking: that what *was* still *is* and *always will be*. The Eucharist of the Church is constructed around this highly poetic "trick of tense."

The Preface Insight

The Eucharistic Prayers of the liturgy are complex artistic creations. For many years the Roman Catholic Church possessed only one of them: the Roman Canon (now Eucharistic Prayer I). This lengthy set of prayers, reserved traditionally to the priest, contains the Consecration and forms the major part of the Mass.[7] The drive since Vatican II to encourage a ritual in which the whole congregation can participate has seen some changes of form to what was once the prayer of the priest alone.[8] But my concern here is not about the shape of this beautiful prayer, but rather about its meaning.

The questions I wish to probe are: When we engage in the prayer of the Eucharist, what is it we imagine we are doing? When the community gathers to tell the story of "the night before he died," what is the point and focus of it all? What does the celebration *mean*? What are we attempting to achieve in the experience? And with what coherent language can we explain ourselves to others (especially our children)?

The Preface to the Eucharistic Prayer functions in the way of a prelude to an orchestral symphony: a premonition of all the symphony's major movements can be found therein. The Church possesses a vast expanse of Preface texts suitable for different occasions and all of them reflect faithfully the patterns of language I will now analyze within one of them: the Preface of Eucharistic Prayer II.[9]

Eucharist Prayer II is a translation (reasonably faithful) of one of the Church's oldest and most treasured such prayers from the year 215 in Rome.[10] One characteristic of this prayer is its brevity and focused language. Its Preface models particularly well one specific pattern of the language of ritual—the interplay of the tenses of verbs—that alerts us to the original meanings of Hebrew (and Christian) worship. This is presented in diagram 4.

The Preface always commences in the present tense, inviting the community to give thanks to God in the great *berakah* song. The community responds, declaring their willingness to be led into such prayer of praise and blessing. The presider then continues this Hebrew-patterned proclamation of the rightness of our joy and praise: "it is our duty and salvation ... to give you thanks through ... Jesus Christ! He is the Word ... "

This is all in the *present tense*. It is a declaration of this community's current sense of appreciation and wonder—because *Jesus is the Word!*

Then abruptly, the prayer changes into *past tense*: Jesus, through whom God *made* the universe, the one *sent* to redeem us, who

Diagram 4.

Tenses in the Preface to the Eucharistic Prayer

Present Tense

The Lord ***be*** *with you.*
And also with you.

Lift up *your hearts.*
We ***lift*** *them up to the Lord.*

Let us give thanks *to the Lord, our God.*
It is right to give him thanks and praise.

Father, it ***is*** *our duty and our salvation,*
always and everywhere
to give you thanks through your beloved Son, Jesus Christ.

He is the Word

Past Tense

through whom you ***made*** *the universe,*
the Savior you ***sent*** *to redeem us.*
By the power of the Holy Spirit
he ***took*** *flesh and* ***was*** *born of the Virgin Mary.*

For our sake he ***opened*** *his arms on the cross;*
He ***put*** *an end to death*
and revealed the resurrection.
In this he ***fulfilled*** *your will*
and ***won*** *for you a holy people.*

Present Tense

And so we ***join*** *the angels and the saints* ***in proclaiming*** *your glory as we* ***sing****:*

Holy, holy, holy Lord, God of power and might,
heaven and earth ***are*** *full of your glory.*
Hosanna in the highest.
Blessed is he who ***comes*** *in the name of the Lord.*
Hosanna in the highest.

took flesh and *was born* of Mary, who on Calvary *opened his arms* and thus *put an end to death, revealed* the meaning of resurrection, and thereby fulfilled God's will and won forever a new people. This presentation of past-tense verbs can mislead a worshipping community into thinking that we are here referring simply to the life of Jesus of Nazareth, that these things all happened in the distant past. We *are* remembering the Jesus of history, the one born of Mary who died one particular day on Calvary and who rose—these things are all true. But when such language is used in a setting of ritual, the use of past tense is a linguistic trick to awaken us to a realization far more beautiful and awesome than any mere event of past times.

For notice how smoothly the transition is then made again into present tense—"and so we join in proclaiming … "—and the community who have listened attentively to this *apparently past story* now reclaims for themselves the proclamation as it continues with "Holy, holy, holy Lord." The one great song of the Preface, beginning in *present tense*, then slipping into *past tense*, now reverts smoothly into *present-tense* singing. If we are not conscious of this poetic process we can fall into thinking that the centerpiece of the song (the references to Jesus in the past tense) are merely literal references to the life he once led. We can be fooled into imagining that all the prayer is talking about is a life lived in Palestine long ago (Jesus of Nazareth). However to read the prayer so literally is to miss the mythic point that the composer of an apparently jumbled set of tenses is trying to make for us. The composer's intention is made lucid if we momentarily cast the whole Preface in the consistent tense with which it begins and ends, as presented in diagram 5.

When the total Preface is cast into a consistent *present tense*, what an amazing perspective on *our lives* is revealed …

The Preface is speaking about us—the language refers to Jesus, but the reality is Jesus *and us*! What we are celebrating and singing about is the reality of our own struggling, yet noble, lives.

- Humanity collaborates with God in the future shape of the world. The universe is still being fashioned—for good or ill—and

Diagram 5.

The Preface to the Eucharistic Prayer in Present Tense

Present Tense

The Lord ***be*** *with you.*
And also with you.

Lift up *your hearts.*
We lift them up to the Lord.

Let us give thanks *to the Lord, our God.*
It is right to give him thanks and praise.

Father, it ***is*** *our duty and our salvation,*
always and everywhere
to give you thanks through your beloved Son, Jesus Christ.

He is the Word
through whom you ***are making*** *the universe,*
the Savior you ***still send*** *to redeem us.*
By the power of the Holy Spirit
he ***takes*** *flesh and* ***is*** *born of the Virgin Mary.*

For our sake he ***opens*** *his arms on the cross;*
He ***is putting*** *an end to death*
and ***revealing*** *the resurrection.*
In this he ***fulfills*** *your will*
and ***wins*** *for you a holy people.*

And so we ***join*** *the angels and the saints*
in proclaiming *your glory as we* ***sing****:*

Holy, holy, holy Lord, God of power and might,
heaven and earth are full of your glory.
Hosanna in the highest.
Blessed is he who comes in the name of the Lord.
Hosanna in the highest.

is very much dependent on the quality of our loving (or unloving) decisions. Jesus was once "sent to redeem us," but who now carries that same redemption forward into the lives of people today? The redemptive presence of love in the world is far, far from completed.

- If in Jesus, God's presence "took flesh" at a certain moment of history, then does it not still take flesh in *our* manner of living and loving—called as we are to embody God's justice and tender mercy? Jesus "was born of Mary" once only, and long ago. So where is Christ being born today? And who is this "Virgin Mary" who gives birth to the presence of Jesus in these times? Surely, we are speaking of *ourselves*, of the faithful and loyal *Church* in its deepest and broadest meaning.

- In the world of today, what is our consciousness of Jesus "still opening his arms on a cross"? Where is it happening? What is our perception of that reality? And whose body is hanging upon it? What is our understanding of this?

- Who are they whose living commitments demonstrate "an end to death," and thus show forth in brilliant light the fullest meanings of "resurrection"? Who today is "fulfilling God's will" and "winning a holy people"?

These beautiful images both challenge and confirm us in our calling as baptized believers.[11] There is nothing irrelevant about this liturgy. It celebrates *our* lives! It announces *our* ennoblement into the calling and consciousness of Jesus: we *are* his life. It is therefore no wonder that such an awesome realization now inspires the community to sing the "Holy, holy, holy" response: the first of the three great Acclamations that are found in every Eucharistic Prayer.

The Three Great Acclamations

In the early centuries, the Eucharist had a variety of names, one of which was simply "the Mystery."[12] In the Greek world of that time, pagan cults of the various heroic gods often performed rituals in worship that were simply called "the mysteries." Members kept details of such activities to themselves, hence one meaning of the term "mysteries": they were not to be lightly shared with outsiders. But a second meaning of the word was more complex, referring to the effect of the secret rituals on those who participated in them. When the ritual of the sun-god was performed, for example, those who actively took part were seen as being taken up into the actual lifecycle of the sun-god invoked. They became part of the deity's life. The ritual was an act of divine participation in which the immortal life of the god was seen as conferred upon those assembled. In this sense, a *mystery* was a story-in-ritual that *lifted participants onto a higher plane of existence*: they became part of the deity.

The early Church had no difficulty with this way of thinking when applied to Jesus. Christian faith was understood basically as a gift for living on a different plane, or for seeing one's life in a different dimension: as an extension of the life and mind of Jesus. The Eucharist could happily be called a "mystery" because it celebrated the belief that in the ritual we are lifted onto a different level of consciousness, invited to see ourselves as the embodiment of Christ in history. In this awareness, one's day-to-day life, one's human suffering and struggle, are seen as a way of participating in the life-giving commitment that characterized Jesus. In terms more religious, one could say that we become the extension of his redemption across times and cultures.

1. The Sanctus Acclamation

In the first major Acclamation of the Eucharistic Prayer, the people proclaim the holiness of God, the sacredness of all creation, and themselves in the mystery of Jesus:

Holy, holy, holy Lord, God of power and might,
heaven and earth are full of your glory.
Hosanna in the highest.
Blessed is he who comes in the name of the Lord.
Hosanna in the highest.

We name creation as sacred, as full of the glory of God. This is a commitment in faith to the goodness of it all. Our gracious task as believers is to render that glory evident.

We then dare to name Jesus as the one "who comes in the name of the Lord." This is a magnificent vision, but let us not miss the underlying realism of this reference to Jesus. For the one "who comes in the name of the Lord" today is ourselves. There is no other. We gather on Sunday to nominate ourselves into the person of Jesus: we are lifted up into that *mysterion*, clothed in that myth of his life and person. On any Sunday, it is *our* lives that we gather to celebrate—references to Jesus are references to *our* lives. This is the whole point and focus of the Christian eucharistic ritual. The mystery is ourselves.

This is why the proper medium of the Eucharist has always been music. Only singing can properly express the joy and sense of wonder that lie at the heart of the mystery we are: *berakah* is a song.

2. The Consecration Acclamation

Just as the Preface plays upon the transition between tenses (what *was* still *is*), so does the text of the Eucharistic Prayer itself. At the core of this priestly prayer, which is mostly centered on the gifts of bread and wine, we find the narrative taken from the Gospel accounts of Jesus' final evening with his disciples. Naturally, it is presented in past tense imagery: "he *took* bread and *gave* you thanks ... *broke* the bread, *gave* it to his disciples, and *said* ... " The same tenses continue throughout the gesture with the cup of wine: "he *took* the cup. Again he *gave* you thanks and praise, *gave* the cup to his disciples, and *said* ... " And just as in the Preface, the tense then reverts to the present form: "Let us proclaim the mystery of faith ... "

Notice that what is then proclaimed is "the mystery" of faith. The assembly acknowledge in their sung response, not simply the whole Hebrew mindset of the relationship between past, present, and future, but that the body given and blood poured out are indeed *mysterion* (an identity for living into which they themselves have been lifted):

"Christ has died..."	"Christ is risen..."	"Christ will come again..."
The past	The present	The future
The story that *was*...	still *is*...	and *always will be!*

It is as if the term "Christ" takes on a different shade of meaning with each part of the Acclamation: Christ has died—Yes! But (in us) Christ is risen—Yes! And through our living of *hesed* and *emet*, Christ will come again—Yes! It is a powerful affirmation of our faith in Jesus, but it is also a marvelous affirmation of the reality we believe ourselves to be: the body and presence of Christ today.

An older Catholic piety sought to express this same sense of the interplay of tenses when it declared that "each Mass was the sacrifice of Calvary over again." We understood that at each Mass we offered Jesus again to God, just as happened on Calvary. This is indeed our Catholic tradition and faith. But what we could not easily grasp was how *we* were connected with that offering. Our analysis of Hebrew ritual teaches us today that the interplay of tenses mentioned above—that what *was*, still *is*, and always *will be*—indicates a view of human history (and therefore of Jesus) that names *his* story as normative for all generations and epochs. In other words, there is only this *one story* through which Christians can find meaning and context for their lives. Each Eucharist *is* about the sacrificial life of Jesus—"my body given, my blood poured out for you." But the Christian boast is that we have come to see ourselves as living in him, as swept up (baptized) into his reality. So that when we offer Jesus, we ourselves are thereby offered in the same gesture.[13] Underlying this profound understanding is the realization of the manner in which we participate not merely in the activities of the ritual (reading, singing, responding), but also in the very reality about which the ritual is speaking: *whose body is today upon the Cross of Jesus?* In a deeply mysterious but nonetheless true sense, the "*holy* and *living* sacrifice" is ourselves.[14]

The implications of this shift in perception are very important. The daily struggle of the Cross is part and parcel of the lives of all in attendance at every Eucharist. The cares and concerns of parents, the uncertainties of the young, the loneliness and grief of the elderly, the whole human web of pain is today's Cross of Christ. Like his, our lives redeem. We are living the redemptive love of Christ: it is who we are. The struggle to realize covenant community in today's world is as demanding as it ever was for Jesus—but our willingness to do it, with whatever resources we possess, is the commitment expressed in our sung Acclamation. It is *ourselves* we give to God, not Jesus. Nor do we give ourselves so much "to God" as to one another in the covenant commitment to build loving community. How could we ever have missed the realism and down-to-earth relevance of this challenging and involving ritual?

3. The Doxology Acclamation

The final segment of every Eucharistic Prayer is called the Doxology.[15] While the Preface functions like a musical prelude, the Doxology has the character of an orchestral reprise. It is too important a summary of the total prayer to ever be altered or changed, and for reasons of its great importance has been traditionally reserved for the presider alone:

Through him,
with him,
in him,
in the unity of the Holy Spirit,
all glory and honor is yours, almighty Father, for ever and ever.

The whole Eucharistic Prayer rises to this climax of images, in which the Church is attempting to put a series of potent images upon the reality of the *mysterion*. Just to ponder the three opening phrases—*through*, *with*, and *in*—opens the mind to the breadth and sweep of the story which ennobles us: Jesus. There is only the one story: it is the story of human hope for today. We ourselves, baptized into Jesus, are that story. This is the faith we have inherited, and it is what we will hand on to succeeding generations of believers. Only through Jesus, with Jesus, and in Jesus do our lives find meaning and we are enabled to live "in the unity of the Holy Spirit"—that is, as a loving and ever-inclusive community of justice.

It seems a great sadness that the whole community gathered for Eucharist is not permitted to make this third Acclamation in one united voice. Unlike the pattern established in the previous two Acclamations, here the community is invited to respond with the merest "Amen!" Composers, rightly sensing the weight of the ritual moment, have attempted to amplify this Great Amen (as it has been called) with repetitions and the addition of Alleluias or similar phrasings. Of even greater interest is the emergence of local customs whereby the presider (sensing the rightness of the moment) invites all present to participate in this encapsulation of the total Eucharistic Prayer. This practice is not lawful, yet history provides ample evidence that emerging custom can produce great changes in liturgical ritual. Considering the timeless truth that nothing educates more surely than rituals that are lucid and involving, perhaps it is time to open the richness of this third Eucharistic Acclamation to the participation of those on whose behalf it is presently proclaimed by the presider.[16]

Why We Gather

We are probing the meaning of the Eucharistic Prayer. Jesus had said, "Do this in remembrance of me." The Church repeats these words at every celebration. This phrase occurs only in Luke's account of the Last Supper (Luke 22:19) and in Paul's reference to the same tradition when writing to the Corinthians (1 Corinthians 11:24). For the phrase, "in remembrance of me," both make use of the same Greek word: *anamnesis*.[17]

It is a word that in Greek culture has a specific meaning. It translates the Hebrew word for a memorial: *zikkaron*. Neither word means what we mean by the simple term *memorial*. Each possesses a distinctive shade of meaning that is of great importance when we speak of the Eucharist as done *in memory of* Jesus.

Anamnesis

A Greek term which means to bring an event *forward* into the present situation; to re-member a past event. Jesus is equivalently saying to the disciples, "Be sure to *carry me forward in your memories* as you repeat this night's ritual."

Zikkaron

A Hebrew term often translated simply as "to remember," but its meaning is far more subtle. It could be described as this: to so portray something *as to make someone else remember.* When used in the context of Hebrew religion it means to act as a community in such a pattern of covenant love *as to make God remember* God's side of the covenant bargain—to be faithful and loyal forever.

Note carefully that when the Hebrew tradition spoke of the covenant and God and *zikkaron*, its understanding arose in a worldview that imagined God as an all-powerful and gracious being separate from creation and responsible for it all. This is not unlike the image of God with which many of us grew up: as if God were an actual person living in a place called heaven and therefore able to "remember" us.

But God is mysterion, a mystery into which we have all been lifted. All of creation and all of us are enwrapped in God. One Hebrew creation tradition speaks of us as made in God's "image" and "likeness" (Genesis 1:26). If we have such an image of God, how does the term *zikkaron* still have meaning?

Whenever a community of believers deliberately interacts with one another in the very same spirit with which Jesus lived, the image of God seeded deep within our beings is released and fills us again. By participating honestly and completely in the activities of our rituals (be they rituals of companionship, of commitment to the poor, of greeting, song, or forgiveness) the divine spirit within us all is enlarged and awakened—the inner spirit of God resonates with the outward experience of the activity. In this sense, God "recognizes" or "remembers" us when we portray the character of the Beloved One, Jesus. Despite our changing images of God, the Hebrew word *zikkaron* may still provide insight into the processes of ritual. What *zikkaron* does do is focus our attention onto our manner of being together as a community committed to living the covenant.

The image is delicate and fanciful, but the realities for which it reaches are crucial and concern the shape and authenticity of eucharistic community. Unless the community portrays the character and person of Jesus, there is (according to the term *zikkaron*) no *remembering* going on. Without overstating the case, we are naming the focus and rationale of eucharistic celebration: to be the real presence of Jesus today. This is the honor given to us; Jesus has become *our* story. The only fitting response? *Berakah!*

For Discussion

1. Eucharist will never become a joyful (sung?) celebration until we approach it with a *eucharistic mind*. Such a mindset is contained in the Hebrew word *berakah*: a cultivated and maturing gratitude—an ever-deepening appreciation—for all we have been given. Without *berakah* there can be no Eucharist.
   Discuss this in the light of your own experience. How central is *berakah* in Catholic spirituality today? When we gather for Mass as a grateful people, what might be the basic focus of our gratitude?

2. "Christ *has* died ...
   Christ *is* risen ...
   Christ *will come* again ... "

   We proclaim a connectedness between the *past*, the *present*, and the *future*. This is the essence of all Christian liturgy. How does this sense of *one story* change your understanding of what we are doing on a Sunday?
   How might this awareness be communicated to children?

3. "He *is* the Word
   through whom you *are making* the universe,

the Savior you *still send* to redeem us.
By the power of the Holy Spirit
he *takes* flesh and *is* born of the Virgin Mary.
For our sake he *opens* his arms on the cross;
He *is putting* an end to death
and *revealing* the resurrection.
In this he *fulfills* your will
and *wins* for you a holy people."

When this Preface (to Eucharistic Prayer II) is cast in a consistently *present tense*, which line most encourages your faith? Try to express whatever perspectives of faith and life are thus opened up for you.

4. "Father, may this Holy Spirit sanctify these offerings.
Let them become the body and blood of Jesus Christ our Lord
as we celebrate *the great mystery*
which *he left us as an everlasting covenant.*"
(Eucharistic Prayer IV)
The Church borrowed the word *mystery* (Greek: *mysterion*) from the Greek culture in which it had taken root. It referred to any ritual whose task was to develop in participants *a consciousness into which they could be lifted.*
How would you speak about being "lifted into the consciousness" of Christ? In what way can it be said that Jesus has "left the mystery to us"?

5. An important Catholic saying used to be: "The Mass is Calvary over again each day."
In what sense do you now understand this to be true?
What does the Eucharist affirm about the lives and struggles of ordinary participants?

6. "Through him, with him, in him … "
These mysterious words summarize the total Eucharistic Prayer. Explore with one another the depths of meaning you now find in them.

7. "Lord, may this *sacrifice*
   which has made *our peace with you*,
   advance the peace and salvation of *all the world*."
   (Eucharistic Prayer III)
   To what "sacrifice" is the prayer making reference?
   How does such a sacrifice make "our peace with you"?
   How does it "advance the peace and salvation *of all the world*"?

CHAPTER SIX

Communities of the Word

In obedience we come,
we are people of the Word [1]

The Jewish covenant was about honoring God, but it would find expression in harmonious human relationships. Matured in the sufferings of Egypt, those twelve struggling tribes of Hebrews began to imagine for themselves a new way of being together. They chose to relate with one another in God's spirit of *hesed* and *emet*. They summarized it in what we know as the Ten Commandments.

We have also seen how this vision was inherited by Jesus, who grew to love his people so deeply that his commitment to *hesed* and *emet* would take him even to the Cross on his people's behalf. His sense of the covenant-to-be-lived was so encompassing, so open even to those who were considered "outsiders" and "sinners," that at his final meal he refers to what he has lived as the *new* covenant. He was prepared to seal it with his blood—so deeply was he committed to its truthfulness.

The story today is no different. The dimensions of human exploitation and loss of trust may indeed be larger today than in Jesus' lifetime, but the realities of personal sin and alienation are the same. The religious task is far from diminished: the Church exists to bring the story of Jesus into a hopeful engagement with struggling and ordinary lives. For we have come to believe that this story, taken on board in faith, will transform us into him, regenerate our energies, and invest our simple lives with meaning, purpose, and hope.

The Sunday Eucharist is a regular commitment to expose our minds and hearts to the Jesus story. It is a ritual for those committed to the story. We come, not privately, but in the company of others of like conviction—for his is a story about the renovation of human *community*. We come to hear the Story: to swallow, do, and become the Story. Each Sunday's set of scriptural readings (the Word of God) focuses on the person of Jesus—whether as intimations of the person he would be (the first reading) or as later reflections on his life by those who believed in him (the second and Gospel readings).[2] The Church now realizes that the Word of God is the core and heartland of all Catholic ritual and life.

Only the Word of God can build Christian community. That crucial turning-around of the human heart, so necessary for true community to happen, can be achieved only by allowing the Word to dissolve the barriers of the mind. Unless I submit my defenses to the assault of God's Word, then I am not willingly vulnerable to repentance, conversion, and growth. Without such personal submission, community cannot grow. Conversion of hearts and minds, a conversion that is personal, continuous, and conscious, is proof that the Word is "alive and active" in any community.[3]

All the sacraments and all gospel activity are simply expressions of the Word. Since Vatican II, the foundation of Catholic life is the Word of God. On the one hand, like Mary (the Church's best self-image), we ponder Scripture privately in our hearts (Luke 2:51).[4] But on the other hand, like the disciples on the road to Emmaus, we build community faith by probing together the Word's application to our lives and times. Remember how they first shared the scriptures with a stranger (Jesus, a lively engagement) and *then* found themselves prompted to invite him for a meal as evening fell (Luke 24:13-35). Like the *old* covenant at Sinai, with its story of journey, of wilderness, and of meeting God, so is the *new* covenant of Jesus presented by Luke. Emmaus describes an Exodus journey—a portrait of yet another Passover—but told now in terms more easily recognizable for communities whose lives are based on the Eucharist of Jesus.

Journey to Emmaus – A Eucharistic Model

For these two disciples, walking from Jerusalem to Emmaus, the wilderness of their lives was a reality. They had built their hopes and dreams on Jesus—now he was dead. Shattered and disillusioned, they were leaving Jerusalem, but were deeply engaged with each other in trying to fathom the meaning of it all:

> ... and they were talking together about all that had happened ... their faces downcast. (Luke 24:14, 17)

What they were struggling with (and faithfully doing so) was the mystery of Jesus' life. What had it all meant? And what were the implications for themselves?

> Our own hope had been that he would be the one to set Israel free. (Luke 24:21)

On joining them, Jesus simply takes them more carefully into the scriptures to see what bearing the Word of God might have on their present circumstance. He does no more than engage their lives with the Word. The enlightenment of the scriptures does have a profound impact on them, but we are only told about it later in the story:

> Did not our hearts burn within us as he talked to us on the road and explained the scriptures to us? (Luke 24:32)

Jesus anoints their lives with the scriptures and they begin to see clearly again. Their experience of themselves—and of their predicament—changed dramatically. No longer "downcast," no longer so caught up in their own problems as to be unable to "recognize him," they now become capable of an unexpectedly gracious act of *hesed* and *emet* on nearing their destination:

> When they drew near to the village ... he made as if to go on; but they pressed him to stay with them saying, "It is nearly evening, and the day is almost over." So he went in to stay with them. (Luke 24:28-29)

The story depicts Jesus as a total stranger, yet one who had shared with them an engagement with the Word of God. It was already late in the day. In an earlier Gospel story, Luke comments:

> It was *late afternoon* when the Twelve came up to him and said, "Send the people away, and they can go to the villages and farms round about to find *lodging* and *food* … "
> (Luke 9:12-17)

This miracle story of the feeding of the crowds is common to Mark, Matthew, and John. The others all mention the crowd's need for *food*, but Luke is the only evangelist to include the need for *lodging* as well. Now here, in the Emmaus story, lodging for the night becomes an issue: "they pressed him to stay with them." One could conjecture that in Luke's mind these two searching disciples were unknowingly living out the very essence of that earlier eucharistic story, the feeding of the crowds.

Given that Luke is fascinated by the theme that life is a journey for us all, the prominence he gives to hospitality in these twinned stories is most significant: *hesed* and *emet* for travelers.

The Emmaus story climaxes with Jesus doing the eucharistic gesture. Luke employs four key eucharistic verbs—the same verbs used in the previous feeding story—to describe what Jesus then did:

> … he *took* the bread and *said the blessing*; then he *broke* it and *handed* it to them. (Luke 24:30)

The Emmaus story tells us that, startled by this so Jesus-like gesture, they *recognized him*. Then, fresh with insight and new energy, they return immediately to Jerusalem to share with their struggling community:

1. "… their story of what had happened on the road … "

2. "and how they had recognized him at the breaking of bread." (Luke 24:35)[5]

Two moments, but within the one eventful story: what had happened on the road (the open-hearted sharing of life's struggle in light of the Word of God) was subsequently ritualized (the breaking of bread). The Word becomes the ritual; the ritual embodies the Word. One event, but two moments. And the story turns on their gracious offer of hospitality to Jesus. This is the point at which the two disciples had themselves "done the Eucharist" and "broken the bread" of their lives by offering him "the lodging" (remember the prominence of this word in Luke's feeding story). Indeed, the disciples' eyes are only fully opened *after* they have shown warm hospitality to a stranger. There are eucharistic lessons in this for all our assembling communities, lessons about gathering and welcoming and the sharing of our lives "on the road."

The story itself is a carefully crafted interplay of Word, of action in response to the Word, and of a ritual of bread and wine that summarizes it all: one story with three interwoven components. Our Sunday ritual is crafted along similar lines:

1. An engagement of the *Word* with *our lives.*

2. The *following action* of offering *hospitality* (prayers of the faithful and the bringing of gifts).

3. The *ritualizing* of that gracious *mentality* when we (like Jesus) "take bread, thank God for it, break it, and give it."

Just as in the Emmaus story, the Sunday experience stands or falls on the strength with which the Word of God engages our real lives. In the wilderness of their circumstance, these two honest disciples "met God" in a new way by daring with a stranger an honest and persistent conversation. The warmth of their subsequent hospitality, the change of heart in them to sense the stranger's need for lodging, was dependent entirely on their readiness to be vulnerable to the scriptures. Within the hospitality of their scriptural discussion along the road, their hearts became companionable and community was being forged. Their subsequent offer of hospitality and food was but a natural extension to that sharing of the Word. It was the Word that turned them around, the Word that changed them.

It is the same with the Eucharist today: to the extent that we work the Word of God into our hearts in a mutual, honest, and respectful sharing of its implications for our lives, to that extent will we become community in Christ. Central and crucial to the meaning of Eucharist—in any community—is that community's engagement with the Word of God.

Built on the Word

It is to the great credit of Vatican II that in its reform of the liturgy the Word of God was reinstated to its rightful prominence in Catholic life. No longer can any sacrament be attempted without a communal involvement with the Word: scriptural readings now encompass all Catholic ritual. It is the Word that informs, the Word that creates life, the Word about which we then proceed to "make sacrament" each time. In terms of the Eucharist, it is no exaggeration to suggest that what we eat in Holy Communion is the Word of God to which we have already listened: we feed on (and take inside ourselves) the gospel story of Jesus. When we thus take his life on board, Jesus lives, Jesus is present. This is the most basic meaning of sacramental presence: when *we* live the Word, *he* lives! As in the liturgy of Exodus 24, our community's *commitment to live the Word* is expressed in the community coming forward to *drink from the cup*. The readings and the act of coming to Communion are not as unconnected as we may have once thought. This crucial insight lies at the heart of the liturgical renewal of recent years and it will have far-reaching consequences for the shape of public worship in years to come. In a challenging sense, the Word of God is the sacrament:

> The celebration of Mass in which the word is heard and the Eucharist is offered and received forms but one single act of divine worship.[6]

An enormity of change in Catholic thinking lies underneath this apparently simple statement. Caught in the aftermath of Vatican II's regeneration of the Sunday ritual, we can easily forget the poverty and minimalism of "the Mass" prior to the council. In those days, Catholics would have seen "the sacrament" as *very* distinct from "the readings." Indeed, the two readings (in Latin) played something of only a preparatory role for the *sacrifice* we associated with the Consecration that followed.[7] Catholicism's focus was with the "sacramental moment" of the Consecration: that was the Presence we recognized. When the words of Consecration were spoken by the priest, Jesus came; prior to that moment, he was not really present. We thought of Jesus' presence in graphic, almost physical terms: Body meant *body* and Blood meant *blood*. In a Catholicism that saw the Scripture readings as of secondary importance to the moment of Consecration, we would have had little or no experience of the "hearts burning within us" as we "talked together on the road" of the meaning of "the scriptures" for our lives. Having "lost the Word," our sense of sacrament was impoverished and our reading of "the real presence of Christ" was non-inclusive of ourselves as community.

Happily, Catholic culture has changed and a broader sense of Christ's presence in the eucharistic celebration—taken as a *whole*—is being recovered. The General Introduction to the Lectionary now asserts that, "the Scriptures are the living waters from which all who seek life and salvation must drink" (no. 5).

And in the same text the Church goes even further, stating that:

> The more profound our understanding of the liturgical celebration, the higher our appreciation of the importance of God's word. (no. 5)

What we are dealing with here is a revolution in Catholic thinking and a total reshaping by Vatican II of our recent and deeply ingrained "tradition." Word and sacrament form *the one reality*. The "sacrifice of the Mass" is not something that refers to Jesus alone; it embraces us as well. To take seriously the Word of God and to commit ourselves to live it together—this is the Church's most traditional meaning for the word "sacrifice."[8] Unless the Word of God becomes the living heart of every Catholic community, we will never grow to appreciate the deepest meaning of this all important word: *sacrifice.*

Whereas we would once have associated the word "sacrifice" with the way Jesus alone gave himself to God (continued at every Mass), we are now confronted by the deeper, more inclusive meaning of the eucharistic "sacrifice": the gift of *ourselves* to God as a community striving—as did he—to live the covenant vision of Exodus. In this striving, it is ourselves we offer, not Jesus. Yet clothing *ourselves* in his story of fidelity (the Word), we rightly *call* ourselves "Jesus." This is simply the bequest Jesus left us: "Do this—*yourselves*—in *my* memory." Every Mass is Calvary over again (as we used to say), but the issue now concerns who is on the contemporary Cross. It is ourselves—and our suffering brothers and sisters. Living "in Jesus," we are the contemporary sacrifice. There is no other. Jesus himself died but once, yet he "was raised from the dead to make us live fruitfully for God" (Romans 7:4).

Is it any wonder that we choose to gather each Sunday, in conscious and appreciative community, to celebrate and thank God for this mysterious dignity (to be "in Christ") that has been so graciously conferred upon us and in which we are allowed to participate? Is it any wonder that the medium of the Eucharist was always meant to be joyful singing? Finally, is it any wonder that Vatican II's primary challenge to us all is to reawaken that sense of "full, conscious, and active participation ... which is demanded by the very nature of the liturgy."[9]

True Sacrifice

Pagan understandings of sacrifice have no place in Christian worship. For us today, in the direct line of Jesus, the most demanding "sacrifice" is to submit ourselves to the Story of his life and to clothe ourselves in his mind. The history of the Church testifies that whenever an individual laid down his or her life in *hesed* and *emet* (martyrdom), they were seen as "reproducing the pattern of Jesus' death" and as completely fulfilling the eucharistic ideal: "This is my body; it is given for you. This is my blood."[10] For this reason, on the precise spot of a martyr's death, an altar would be built on which the faithful could commemorate this supreme conjunction of Eucharist and life.

The sacrifice of the Mass confronts all of us with the cost of submitting to the Story of Jesus, God's Word. When we clothe ourselves in that Story, Jesus lives. When we choose to become the community of Christ in today's world, the cost to each of us will be real: it is the sacrificing of our independent spirits on behalf of others.

The prophet Malachi called this the "pure offering" that alone is acceptable to God and which will be offered "from farthest east to farthest west" (Malachi 1:11).[11] Jesus speaks of worshipping God "in spirit and truth" (John 4:23), and that "anyone who does the will of God ... is my brother and sister and mother" (Mark 3:31-35). The Church, prior to Vatican II, had enshrined Malachi's "pure offering" within the Roman Canon Prayer as the "rational sacrifice": the submission of our minds, hearts, and lives to the gospel story. When talking of the Eucharist as a sacrifice, this is what the Church's best tradition has always had in mind.[12] But in the post-Vatican II form of that ancient prayer, now called Eucharistic Prayer I, we pray (before the Consecration):

> Bless and approve our offering;
> make it acceptable to you,
> an offering in *spirit and in truth* ...

And immediately following the Consecration:

> ... we offer you, God of glory and majesty,
> this holy and *perfect sacrifice*:
> the bread of life
> and the cup of eternal salvation.

When the Church says that the Mass is a sacrifice, something very down-to-earth is meant. There is a mysticism involved, but of a very basic kind: to courageously open my heart—here amongst my companions in faith—to the gospel challenge to be a community for the world in the spirit of a living Jesus. In other words, to live together the Word we hear. The letter of James has a way of putting it directly:

> Humbly *welcome the Word* which has been *planted in you* and can save your souls. But you must *do what the Word tells you* and *not just listen to it* and deceive yourselves. Anyone who listens to the Word and takes no action is like someone who *looks at his own features in a mirror* and, once he has *seen what he looks like*, goes off and immediately *forgets it*. But anyone who looks steadily at *the perfect law of freedom and keeps to it*—not listening and forgetting, but putting it into practice—will be blessed in every undertaking. (James 1:21-25)

The Gospel of each day's liturgy is the mirror of who we are at our most profound level. The stories of how Jesus lived and interacted with people reflect back to us our deepest possibilities. In a true sense the stories in the Gospels are not strictly about Jesus of Nazareth at all—they are about us, about all humanity, about human growth and maturity, about passing-over into God. If we cannot see this startling truth then we will never grasp why each Sunday the Church puts the Gospel stories before us. We go to Mass to look into the mirror, to re-mind ourselves of who we truly are as human persons. For us, Jesus is "the perfect law" and the way he lived his life is a portrayal of "the law of freedom."

Each Sunday's Gospel segment presents a portrait of how our community can live into God: we *listen* to it, we *pay attention* to it, we profess our *obedience* to it: "We shall do everything that Yahweh has said; we shall obey" (Exodus 24:7). The point is to realize that Jesus is "what the Lord has spoken," the utterance of God, the living, breathing realization of the divine seed planted within us all. If in his Story we see God made visible, we also see ourselves in that same moment ...

The Eucharistic Mystery

This vision of what the eucharistic celebration is about is noble and persuasive, but the realities it speaks of are sacrificial in the extreme. The formation of a faith community, one that truly reflects

THE EUCHARISTIC MYSTERY

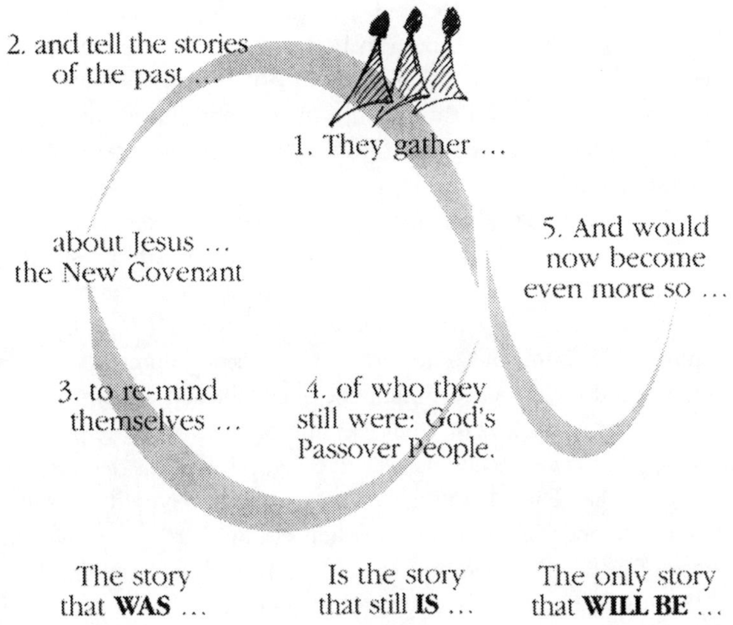

1. They gather ...

2. and tell the stories of the past ...

about Jesus ... the New Covenant

3. to re-mind themselves ...

4. of who they still were: God's Passover People.

5. And would now become even more so ...

The story that **WAS** ...

Is the story that still **IS** ...

The only story that **WILL BE** ...

the gospel's vision of *hesed* and *emet*, will cost all of us not less than everything. Again, the letter of James spells this out in detail:

> My brothers and sisters, do not let *class distinction* enter into your faith in Jesus Christ, our glorified Lord. Now suppose a man comes into your synagogue, well-dressed and with a gold ring on, and at the same time a poor man comes in, in shabby clothes, and you take notice of the well-dressed man, and say, "Come this way to the best seats"; then you tell the poor man, "Stand over there" or "You can sit on the floor by my foot-rest." In making this *distinction among yourselves* have you not used a corrupt standard? (James 2:1-4)

It is almost as if James is using the current idiom, exhorting us not to even try to put together in our minds the notion of faith and the making of distinctions! They simply cannot go together: they are opposites, contradictories. It is of the very essence of Jesus to be consciously inclusive, both in how we live and in how we see people. This sense of the shared nobility of all is what Jesus meant by covenant. It formed the basis of his life and lies at the core of Christian religious experience. The Church's technical term for this is "holy communion."

When we "receive Holy Communion" we are receiving into ourselves that way of being together—*without favoritism*. By standing and approaching Holy Communion, I publicly commit myself to step into a *holy community*. But I am not stepping only into this community around me here, not just the local community assembled around me: it is a commitment to consider *all people* as holy, *all people* as noble and *all reality* as impregnated with the presence of God. This is to "receive Jesus": to take on board his deepest perceptions, to take inside oneself his way of being alive. In this sense, going to Holy Communion is a ritual committing me to live that sense of justice that is found in God alone and that is exemplified in the stories of how Jesus lived. This is why the Church calls Jesus the justice of God: he puts things right, portrays those patterns-for-living that alone mature us, and demonstrates a way of interacting and of "seeing" one another that creates liberating relationships.

James names all of this "faith": it concerns the formation of community without favoritism, without distinctions. Ever practical, he then describes in vivid detail some crucial implications: curbing the tongue, watching our language, controlling how we speak of others. This is the cost—the sacrifice entailed—of Christ-like community. It demands we keep a close watch on jealousy and ambition (the roots of human disharmony). It calls for a stand against unjust wages. It presumes a growing awareness of the wrongfulness of comfortable and luxurious lives in the midst of oppression and suffering.

For James, submission "to the Word that is planted in you" is an earthy reality. While he himself does not mention the Eucharist he speaks about faith in a language close to that used by Paul: in terms of community and social responsibility. James is very focused when it comes to what makes faith real:

> If one of the brothers or one of the sisters is *in need of clothes* and has *not enough food to live on*, and one of you says to them, "I wish you well; keep yourself warm and eat plenty," *without giving them these bare necessities of life*, then what good is that? In the same way faith: if good deeds do not go with it, is quite dead. (James 2:15-17)

According to this line of thinking, there is nothing more dangerous than to listen with open and willing heart, in the company of like-minded people, to the Word of God as expressed in the Gospels. It must change us. It makes demands of us. The deepening of our living of *hesed* and *emet* is never completed, but is always newly challenged in the changing circumstances of everyday living. In this sense, to apply the Word in a living way to our contemporary world setting we need one another's experience and wisdom, we need one another's insight, courage, and support. What the Eucharist is about is the formation of a deliberately-intended community that is washed in the spirit of Jesus. In this noble but pain-filled process there are several levels of personal sacrifice involved:

1. To be a willing participant in this local community, whatever its faults and failings, is *sacrificial*. The simple commitment to join with this mix of humanity in the pursuit of the gospel ideal is far more challenging than any of us would like to admit.

2. To sign oneself over into this process of gospel formation is to become a willing participant in conversations that work the gospel's challenge into our shared lives. This can be a demanding and *sacrificial* pathway.

3. It is as practical as the decisions one makes as to where one sits each time one attends the Eucharist and with whom does one share the Sign of Peace each week? To move beyond one's personal zone of comfort in this way is *sacrificial*.

4. The commitment to "building the faith of others" prompts me to attend the Eucharist with regularity. To be thus "body given for you" is profoundly *sacrificial.*

5. It is about joining in the ritual and singing. It is about learning to listen with respect to the life experiences of others as we ponder the gospel's impact on how we live. It is about being prepared to participate in a way that is as full, as conscious, and as active as one's circumstances allow. All of which is *sacrificial.*

6. It involves a commitment (as best as one can) to the community's project of bringing the real presence of Jesus to the cities, the streets, the political processes of our time. It is to be a participant in the gathering of gifts for the poor (the collection) and perhaps to be called into the ministry of distributing them (outreach). It is a commitment to lay one's gifts, talents, skills, and education at the service of local need (to whatever degree one can). This is profoundly *sacrificial.*

This sense that *we are the sacrifice* has always been present within the Church's eucharistic prayers, the sense that our obedience to the Word of God constitutes the offering we make to God: as Jesus lived obediently, so shall we. For this reason, Eucharistic Prayer III calls such an offering a "living sacrifice"—a most unusual conjunction of two terms. It is even clearer in Eucharistic Prayer IV where we read:

> Lord, look upon *this sacrifice* which you have given to your Church …
> gather all who share this one bread and one cup
> *into the one body of Christ, a living sacrifice* of praise.

The Mass is a sacrifice, true; but becoming a community driven by the gospel story is what the sacrifice is all about. We therefore come to the Eucharist as an opportunity of using the ritual to commit ourselves to the living of the gospel story we will hear. The Word is the sacrament. The sacrament is the acted-upon Word. They are but two moments of the one, same experience called worship:

When this word is *proclaimed* in the Church and *put into living practice*, it *enlightens* the faithful ... and draws them into *the entire mystery* of the Lord as *a reality to be lived*.[14]

Doing Well the Word

From what has been said, a fruitful involvement of our congregations in the eucharistic mystery depends crucially on the quality with which we celebrate the Word of God. The Readings, impacting on the consciousness of the assembly, make possible the following sacramental act. The issue, in most Sunday celebrations, lies in making sure that the Readings actually do impact on the congregation. In recent years, much good work has gone into this, including structured courses for lectors and musicians (whose different ministries must particularly dovetail for the Readings to be effective). However, on the level of the local parish community, much still needs to be done and some basic perspectives (coming from the Church itself) still need to be integrated if the participation of our congregations in the Word is to be "full, conscious, and active."

1. The Unity of the Gospel and First Readings

The Gospel is the key to the Readings. The First Reading is chosen to throw light upon the Gospel Reading. They should be considered in tandem. In the Roman mind, the responsive-style Psalm is considered part of the First Reading (like the second half of it). The Response is that segment of the First Reading in which the people can participate (in the musical response phrase).

The Gospel Reading presents us with some aspect of Jesus (or his life) that is intended to anoint our own lives with meaning. It may be an aspect of Jesus' person (or attitude to life) that deeply challenges us. Either way, it is on the person of Jesus that one should concentrate when trying to gauge the Gospel's significance for this community. Gone are the times when Catholics invariably identified with the "downside" of any Gospel story: seeing ourselves, for example, as the prodigal son, or the wayward sinner, or the lost sheep. Such images may occasionally be the desired focus of a liturgy, but in general terms, on any particular Sunday the Church is asking the community to "put on the mind and heart of Christ," so our attention should focus on the ennobling image of who he was, of how he lived. Something of this aspect of Jesus will be found in the First Reading and often the prayer of the Responsorial Psalm will further reinforce such a focus.

So first we look for the graciousness within the Gospel, the graciousness with which to encourage one another into living the reality of Christ today. Those attending the Eucharist come needy, and all of us are struggling in our lives. We come to the Eucharist for heart and encouragement. One primary task of the celebration is *to build one another* into the faith of Jesus.

Well prior to the commencement of the celebration, those who are involved in major ministry roles should be clear on the focus of this particular celebration: What aspect of Jesus' life (that is, of *our* community's life) are we celebrating today? Musicians, readers, presider, and perhaps eucharistic ministers must be part of such clarity—otherwise the performance of their ministry may well interfere with the transparency of the ritual.

For example, the presider needs to be fully conscious of the Gospel's focus, so that the introductory rites and the subsequent Eucharistic Prayer are presented in harmony with that focus.[15] The readers need to be fully aware of what elements within the scriptures call for emphasis.[16]

Musicians particularly must work with great sensitivity to the desired outcome of the Word of God. Music is the privileged language through which the congregation most fully participates and grows toward the consciousness being cultivated by the Word. The Responsorial Psalm is critical in this experience. A community with a repertoire of established, loved responses (some of rejoicing, some of petition, some of lamentation and sorrow, some of commitment) is far more likely to know them by heart and to pray them when sung, than a community that attempts a new response each week. Unless people can pray the response from the heart, the attempt at singing is only damaging the impact of the Word.

2. The Second Reading

A perception, thirty years after Vatican II, is that we present far too much Scripture each Sunday. This may reflect more on our *manner* of presenting the Readings as much as their quantity. Even so, the Second Reading has usually been chosen separately from the Gospel/First Reading combination.[17]

It is not my position to encourage liturgical vandalism, but some judicious ways of using the Second Reading might be considered, especially in light of some major principles laid down by the Church itself in the General Instruction on the Roman Missal:

> It is ... of the greatest importance that the celebration of the Mass ... be so arranged that everyone—ministers and people—may take their own proper part in it ... The best way to achieve this will be to consider the *particular character and circumstances of the community*, and then organize the details of the celebration in a way that will lead them to full, active, and conscious participation.[18]

If our communities are finding the amount of Scripture difficult to digest on a Sunday, then surely some local, creative response is sensible? Especially when the same document goes on to comment:

> Hence all possible care should be taken that, from the rites and ceremonies proposed by the Church, those should be chosen which, in view of individual and local circumstances, will best foster active participation and meet the needs of the faithful.[19]

If the Church is calling us to a mature preparation of each celebration—driven by the need to foster the community's fullest participation and spiritual welfare—then perhaps we need to be more courageous in using our local authority and leadership? And if the Second Reading punctuates the intended unity of flow between the First and Gospel Readings, offering little in the way of crafting a unified sense of this liturgy's gospel challenge, then why not find creative ways of using that Second Reading more effectively (such as relocating it occasionally)?

As a measured reflection *after Holy Communion*, the insights of the New Testament letters can sometimes work marvelously in setting the consciousness of the community toward its mission out in the world. There is a precedent for locating a reading here: the so-called *Last Gospel* (John's prologue) of the Tridentine Mass.

Further, an arresting proclamation—by a lector—of one or two key sentences from the Second Reading can frequently set up the Christian consciousness immediately prior to the commencement of the *Gathering Song*. Likewise, a short segment (perhaps the same key sentence or two) can sharpen the attention immediately prior to the *Missioning Song* that concludes the celebration. In practice, the Second Reading proves far more adaptable than either the First or Gospel Readings for such usage.[20]

3. Fostering the Readership

The ministry of presenting the Word is of critical significance in a celebration, second only to the role of the presider. The whole sacrament, the total ritual, depends on the effectiveness with which the Word is proclaimed. Indeed, in any parish without a resident priest, the importance of the lector is even more enhanced. Within the Catholic tradition of worship, traditions of proclamation are not in place: we are virtually building a new ministry and skill. Unless there is an unexpected change in Church attitudes to priesthood and the Eucharist, many parishes in the near future will be more dependent on the quality of our lectors than ever before. For part of the reader's skill is homiletic. Anyone who proclaims a reading in Church is doing so with an eye to its meaning-for-living (which is the purpose of the homily). Does the ministry of readership have the high profile it deserves amongst us? Or have we so burdened ourselves with such a multiplicity of readers (seeing the numbers involved as an indication of what the Church meant by participation) that the resulting presentation of most readings is either flat, uninspiring, or non-engaging of the congregation?[21] The Church's own words are deeply challenging:

> It is necessary that those who exercise the ministry of reader, even if they have not received institution, be *truly qualified* and *carefully prepared so* that the faithful may develop a *warm and living love for Scripture from listening* to the sacred texts read.[22]

When we remember that for most Catholics their only contact with the Word of God occurs in the Sunday ritual, the importance of delivering it so as to instill—over time—that "warm and living love of Scripture" becomes paramount. Perhaps we are on the edge of developing a specific spirituality of readership, almost a vocation undertaken by the reader, on behalf of the wider community, to so immerse themselves in the Word of God as to render their Sunday service of it inspiring and compelling.

4. Working the Word

In liturgies of great occasion, or in the cathedrals of the country, the presentation of Readings can have more impact than is generally the case on ordinary Sundays and in parish churches. In many situations, the Word of God is not working well. Not infrequently—and despite the best efforts of those who compiled the Lectionary—our communities are faced with Gospel passages or First Readings that are opaque, dense in the extreme, and unrelated to the daily lives of today's people. The Church, however, is not likely to radically recast the Lectionary in the near future, so we must work with what we have. Yet the question remains: How do we work the Word of God effectively into the life of this assembly?

Whatever process we come up with to engage the assembly with the Word of God, one piece of advice from the Church's wisdom is worth remembering:

> The liturgy of the word *must* be celebrated in a way that *fosters meditation*; clearly, any sort of *haste that hinders reflection* must be avoided. The dialogue between God and his people … demands *short intervals of silence, suited to the assembly*, as an opportunity to take the word of God *to heart* …[23]

In the best of Catholic liturgy, silence plays a prominent part. Indeed, many who knew the majesty of the Tridentine liturgy would rue the lack of silence within many of today's celebrations. We are also a culture unused to silence, unsure how to use it to effect. The recovery of a sense of silence would do much to replenish the richness of our rituals (the Eucharist included). But the silences have to be focused and play a constructive part in the overall experience of the celebration. Unless congregations are taught how to ponder, how to listen, and how to deepen the appreciation of any Reading within the ensuing silence, then the process of silence will become just "one more thing" to be done within an already busy ritual.

In the matter of silence, we are dealing with the contemplative aspect of a celebration. It is both a willingness to get oneself inside the text and some simple techniques for doing so—a period of total silence being one of them. Congregations can be taught the ways of being silent as easily as an individual is taught the techniques of prayer and retreat. The goal is to create within the church an atmosphere of attentive, focused pondering. The possibilities for silence differ from occasion to occasion and (naturally) there must be a realism to all this, especially in congregations composed of younger families. But even in such cases, perhaps a carefully phrased question—followed by a moment for reflection—is one way of doing so. The Prayer of the Faithful provides a model that might profitably be followed. Indeed, a series of simple and focused questions—leaving time for the assembly to ponder the question and perhaps to share something of one's insight with those alongside—might be a structure as helpful for the homily as a presentation solely by the presider.

Also, is there any reason not to insert short pauses during the actual Reading (and not just between the Readings)? Once a congregation becomes accustomed to the process (as the way we do things around here), our capacity to make good use of the silence would improve. And, of course, were the Second Reading to be relocated (or abbreviated), there would be time available for a more measured approach to the whole presentation of the Word.

The possibilities are limited only by our imagination. Catching the sense of what the Church sees as important in presenting the Word (pace, silence, and moments of meditation appropriate to the community) is the major step in renovating how we experience the Readings each week.[24]

5. The Prayer of the Faithful

The depth of our listening to the Word of God is the stimulus for turning our hearts and minds *outward* in concerned prayer for the Church and world. It is as if the Prayer of the Faithful is the first measure of our response to the Readings. Prior to Vatican II we had no experience of such a deeply traditional prayer (it had been lost in the process of history).[25]

It is therefore understandable that as we reacquire this treasured moment of the ritual, intentions are presented to the community that have been crafted and prepared long before the day and frequently by authors not belonging to the community. It may be time to question the wisdom of this process (almost an imposition of prayer intentions from outside the praying community).

Might it not be possible that the leadership of such important prayer might be the ministry of a few gifted people from within the assembled community? Especially if the prayer is intended to be *of the faithful who have just listened to the Word of God together?* Might this be an extension of the role of lector? Of those whose service to the community lies in the presentation and processing of the Word of God? There could be then a certain *spontaneity* to the petitions, a capacity to connect the whole prayer to the lives and concerns of the "faithful" who constitute this community. Nor would the immediacy of the prayer prove a great difficulty, provided we followed the Church's best pattern for praying such petitions (the Bidding Prayers of Good Friday). Each segment of the prayer is constructed as follows:

A. Statement of petition (very brief):

"Let us pray for the Holy Father … "

or

"Let us pray for the sick … "

or

"Let us pray for those who govern us … "

B. Period of silence for personal prayer:
Sufficiently lengthy for the person conducting the prayer to also be immersed comfortably in the same process as the assembly.

C. Common (sung) prayer in summary:
Proclamation: "Let us pray to the Lord ... "
Response: "Lord, we ask you hear our prayer ... "

The briefest naming of the petition (or persons for whom we pray) avoids the wordiness of much that is currently occurring. Nor is this prayer a time for lengthy, didactic statements about issues of concern—it is a time for personal prayer (the silence) and support from the assembly for that (the sung response). It might well be a time (depending on the prayerfulness of whoever is naming the petitions) to color the prayer with echoes in word or phrase of the liturgy's Gospel Reading. In this way, the connection between the Word we have heard and the resultant concern for the world is reinforced.

6. Seeding the Eucharistic Prayer

One of the presider's roles is to ensure that the Word of God flows into the consciousness with which the assembly celebrates the sacrament. If all we have been saying is true (that the Word is an essential ingredient of the sacrament) then it would be well to have each celebration impregnated with elements of the Word as it unfolds. This is not as difficult as it sounds—but it does demand of the presider the capacity to lead the Eucharistic Prayer and the Communion ritual while keeping clearly in mind the focus generated during the liturgy of the Word.

This can be as simple as treasuring some key word or phrase from the Readings and readmitting them at timely moments during the subsequent ritual. A selection of the following can be introduced by the judicious use of such a key word or phrase:

1. The Prayer of the Faithful
2. The Collection and Presentation of Gifts
3. The Commencement of the Preface
4. The Great Acclamation after the Consecration
5. The Lord's Prayer and Sign of Peace
6. The Fraction Rite
7. The Postcommunion Prayer
8. The Blessing and Dismissal

As well, during the actual delivery of whatever Eucharistic Prayer is chosen, a reference back to the key Gospel image of the day can be woven rather easily into the fabric of the text itself (with little risk of damage to the poetic flow of the prayer).

Such a conscious application of the Word, on the part of the presider, will only reinforce the impression in the minds of the assembly that this is a conscious, deliberate celebration, indeed a *living* Word. Anointing the eucharistic ritual with some echo of the Readings in this way usually results in the congregation experiencing the liturgy with a clearer focus and attention to what is actually occurring. Yes, it can be clumsily done or even overdone—but the opportunity of thus amalgamating the sacrament and the Word would seem to outweigh other ritualistic concerns. Whenever the Eucharistic Prayer is thus prayed in the obvious consciousness of the Word that was shared, the sung eucharistic responses of the people seem to take on renewed energy and meaning.

The ultimate outcome of any eucharistic celebration is the formation of a community committed to living the covenant in the manner in which Jesus gave himself to its fulfillment. In the eyes of the Gospel writers, Jesus was the Word in full embodiment, the ultimate expression of what *hesed* and *emet* mean in human life. In Communion, Jesus is the Word we eat and in turn we become that same Word in today's world. This is the Mystery into which we have been lifted, the reason for our joy and gratitude. Perhaps the final word belongs to the Eucharistic Prayer itself:

We thank you for counting us worthy
to stand in your presence and serve you.

For Discussion

1. Luke's story of the Feeding of the Crowd (9:12-17) is the only one to mention the crowd's need for *lodging* as well as for *food*. After the resurrection, his story of the journey to Emmaus could be said to focus on the issue of Christian *hospitality*—the disciples pressed the stranger (Jesus) to share their home.
   Where do you see your community challenged in terms of such *hospitality?*
   Are there implications for how our communities *gather* and *welcome* on a Sunday?

2. The Word of God *creates* and *nourishes* the sacrament: Christian communities are built only upon the Word of God.
   When we go to Sunday Eucharist, what is it we actually go there to *do*? What is the point and focus of it all?

3. To take seriously the Word of God and to commit ourselves to its living—this is the Church's most traditional meaning to the word *sacrifice*.
   Discuss with one another your understanding of this statement.

4. We named the presence of Jesus in the bread, but could not name it in ourselves. We created for ourselves a sacred object—the host—and never tasted the full sacredness of being an obedient, searching community in Christ. We read the Emmaus story, but never plumbed the reality of which it spoke: that trio of travelers *became community while struggling with the Word of God for their lives.*
   What application does this have for your own situation?

5. Imagine you are participating in a normal Sunday celebration of the Eucharist. Being realistic, what helpful suggestions can you make to ensure that the Word of God in the readings can impact more powerfully on the lives of all attending? Discuss.

CHAPTER SEVEN

The Long Journey Home

So I leave my boats behind
leave them on familiar shores,
set my heart upon the deep,
follow you again, my Lord[1]

So, where to from here?

The thrust of Vatican II's reform of the Mass was to simplify and focus the eucharistic rituals so that the participation of the whole congregation—priest, ministers, and people—could be *full*, *active*, and *conscious*.

For some of us, the term *participation* suggested an increased busyness on the part of many during the Eucharist. In the past thirty years, we have seen the multiplication of activities associated with the presentation of any Sunday celebration: liturgical planners, eucharistic ministers, readers, musicians, cantors, commentators, ushers, and selected participants in the presentation of the gifts. Yet, in the Church's mind, participation means something far more profound than a mere increase in the number of people doing things.

The basic meaning of participation (as used by the Second Vatican Council) is that all who are present *participate in the meaning and substance of what is happening at the Eucharist.* In other words, that those present be swept up into the mystery of gratitude, self-giving, and joy that the ritual—remembering the appreciative, dedicated, joyful Jesus—is attempting to embody. It means to see one's life as a graced, integral part of the reality we call Jesus. In the mind of the council, participation is about a liturgy unmistakable in its meaning: God has lifted our simple, unspectacular lives into the awesome mystery of Jesus—this is the clarity of consciousness with which the Church wishes to anoint us. Accordingly, the ritual of the Eucharist was changed with this in mind: to enhance the possibility of participation. The Church desires that the ritual be so persuasive as to be irresistible, so engaging as to be involving, yet so simple as to be transparently revealing of the mysterious presence of Jesus continued through us.

> This is why the language of celebration became the language of the congregation. Why the priest now faced the people so that everything could be seen. And why words and prayers were now to be spoken aloud, not silently and privately. Such changes concerned transparency—an attempt to make clearer the *meaning* of the rituals.

In this sense, participation is something that happens to the *total* congregation—it is not measured by numbers involved in ministries (however good a development that might be). Rather, participation is measured by the *quality of insight* gained through involvement in the ritual; it is considered to have occurred when the mystery being celebrated has moved the whole body of people to a new level of consciousness as believers. Such participation is achieved through rituals that engage those present, that hold their attention, and carry them forward into a new dimension of awareness about life. It is, therefore, a matter of justice that the Church employs rituals that are capable of satisfying the people's right to the fullest participation in the mystery being enacted.

Unless people *experience the ennoblement* of their lives (called the mystery of Jesus) then they have not *participated* in the liturgy. The lack of a deliberate education into this awareness lies at the heart of our current liturgical problem: we do not know what we are about.

There are two ways of going about such a catechesis of the people: by direct teaching (seminars, adult formation programs, courses in liturgy), and by allowing a truly effective ritual to engage the people's lives each Sunday.

In other words, the liturgy itself will educate.[2] Both levels of catechesis are crucial if we are to move forward as a worshipping Church.

We will briefly examine a few examples that bear this out.

1. Holy Communion

We have inherited a fragmented ritual of Holy Communion. People are generally unaware of why there are two species of reception: bread *and* wine, Body *and* Blood. A simplistic sense that in both we are "receiving Jesus" is just not sufficient. The meanings for life that lie within these two rich symbols are generally not well understood.

What is needed, on the one hand, is a deliberate education of our congregations in the scriptural origins and meanings of the Body and Blood, for we have lost that historical grounding. Such an education in the root meanings of Body and Blood would do much to restore our sense of the symbolic (that is, sacramental) reality with which we are dealing.

On the other hand, and at the same time, our rituals of consecration, distribution, and reception of bread and wine must be experienced as reflecting the richness about which we are speaking. Some of this is in place in terms of the bread we use (although this varies from place to place) and our growing familiarity with the Cup. Yet practical issues of distribution remain—especially in terms of Cup hygiene. As well, the continuing use by many of the tabernacle as a store of hosts available on Sundays for the ritual itself must pass into history.

2. Bringing Forward the Gifts

Because bread and wine—carried forward and then consecrated—are (according to the Gospel stories) a compellingly clear expression of our being the compassion (and Real Presence) of Jesus today, then should we not pay closer attention to this ritual of bringing forward the gifts?

How can we maximize the involvement and contribution of all present in this important ritual of generosity that sets up the meaning of the subsequent procession for Holy Communion?

How can we make lucid the connection of this presentation of gifts with the poor? It is this connection with the poor of today's world that generates the community's weekly sense of being the Real Presence of Christ.[3] Perhaps the minimalism and non-involving nature of this ritual of generosity is costing us much in terms of eucharistic meaning. How can we better integrate into the procession of gifts the collection of monies just completed? As well, how do we ensure that the congregation understands that such a collection is destined for the poor?

3. The Eucharistic Prayer

The Eucharistic Prayer remains non-participative for most congregations. The Sanctus, the Acclamation, and Great Amen can seem the bare minimum of involvement for them. Through most of this important phase of the Eucharist—where identity in Christ is the issue—the people remain mostly silent onlookers. Recent developments in the design of recurring responses (whether sung or spoken) are clear and happy attempts to address this evident need.[4]

However, if the crux of the Eucharistic Prayer is that the *whole community* is called into the mind and person of Christ—and that the *whole community* makes the ennobling Christ-commitment to the world of today—then why could it not be possible for the people to join in common voice with the priest at certain key moments of this magnificent prayer?

Does it in any way undermine the role of the priest if the people are *led* by that presider in the recitation of a key prayer—for example, in the praying of the climax to the Eucharistic Prayer: "Through him, with him, and in him … "? Or is it entirely beyond reason for the congregation assembled in Jesus to repeat aloud (after the priest has spoken them), the very words of Consecration?

If our people are to wear the liturgy's deepest meanings and break through into the consciousness we desire for them, then surely we can find prayerful and reverent ways of allowing them to claim a greater stake in this heartland of the Eucharist. Such a change needs careful preparation—this is no place for an increase in unauthorized experimentation. Yet, for the sake of a participation that is eloquent and formative of the eucharistic mind, is it not possible to consider a thoughtful and approved recasting of the current ritual?

4. Use of the Scriptures

The Word of God is what ultimately converts and constructs the local community. A profound catechesis (and change of heart) is needed if the scriptures are again to play this central role in Catholic life. Circumstances of inadequate numbers of priests might be forcing the issue for us. Yet the tendency is already apparent to opt for truncated Communion services instead of the more expansive—and demanding—option of liturgies of the Shared Word.

Just as importantly, the sheer volume of Scripture readings each Sunday can militate against a community's ability to take to heart the Word and to nourish their lives upon it. Have we the courage to simplify the presentation of the readings and to build into the *breaking of the Word* some well-tested but simple processes of adult faith sharing? A parish without a priest for celebration provides an ideal opportunity for such an enriching development. Communities of religious are already discovering the *eucharistic* dimensions of such an option in place of their (no longer available) daily Eucharist. But there is even more of a challenge: can we explore uncomplicated ways of shaping both the presentation of the readings and the subsequent homily time so that the whole experience becomes *an involving, homiletic process of insight and personal faith experience?*

Here and throughout this book, we are speaking about a shift in the ownership of the eucharistic ritual, a shift from something that is generated from the altar (priestly dominant) to a ritual that occurs around the table (priestly led but people owned). Such a shift is delicate, but it has surely already been set in train by the liturgical reforms of the Second Vatican Council. What is involved is a re-imagining of priesthood as being inclusive of all God's faithful people and of the liturgy as the joyful weekly recommitment of such a priestly people to the vision of living the covenant—which is called by us, "Jesus." It means that the daring reforms instituted by the Council must be carried through with courage to their completion—lest our people continue to walk away from rituals that are uninvolving and irrelevant to their lives. The task is to recover the heart and core of what liturgy and the Eucharist are all about. It is to admit that from where we now stand, and on the evidence of people's current experience of the eucharistic ritual, we are engaged on nothing less than a long journey home.

NOTES

Chapter 1

1 From "The Galilee Song," in the collection *Everything I Possess* (1981).

2 See the beautiful reference to Jesus in Hebrews (4:15): he is "not incapable of feeling our weaknesses with us, but has been put to the test in exactly the same way as ourselves, apart from sin" (4:15). Sin consists in saying no to the constant call in all our hearts to live more fully the graciousness of God. Jesus never said no. It cost him his life.

3 A free translation of Luke 1:69, as crafted for "The Morning Canticle" in my music recording *Kindly Light* (1992).

4 A free translation based on "The Morning Canticle," also called "The Benedictus," an early Christian hymn of blessing and gratitude written into Luke's Gospel some time after the year eighty. Most probably he joined two distinct hymns that were already being sung in Christian gatherings. These two hymns were Jewish in style and composition and are precious, primary symbols of our Christian faith.

5 From the Greek *ex-odos*, in which ex- signifies "outwards," "across," or "over," and *odos* means "journey." Hence the sense of transition, the "journey over into."

6 Although scholars dispute whether the actual meal Jesus celebrated that night was indeed a Passover meal, nevertheless all the Gospel writers insist on linking the occasion with the Feast of Passover (during which Jesus died). The Gospels are adamant that the Last Supper and his death occurred "in the time of Passover" and that they must be understood in that context.

7 Psalm 137 as recast in my song "By the Rivers of Babylon," in the collection *Kindly Light*.

8 Sadly, the term "covenant," so central to the faith inherited by Jesus, is not yet common currency among Catholics. Perhaps, in our individualistic version of the faith (personal salvation, personal sacraments), it was too communal a word to have held our attention. It represents, however, the core of the current struggle to reclaim the sacraments and our rituals of worship.

9 Hebrews 5:8 says of Jesus: "he learnt ... through his sufferings." It is a phrase of great encouragement to us all. The writer thus names the source of Jesus' wisdom and compassion, while at the same time noting that Jesus matured in the process of his living.

10 The First Letter of Peter (2:9) will take up these foundational words and apply them to the Church: "a chosen race, a kingdom of priests, a holy nation, a people to be a personal possession ... of God."

11 The Commandments are no final word on morality. They represent a stage of development within Israel's history of moral growth. Inconsistent applications of one or other commandment can be found within the Old Testament. Jesus was thus able to say: "Do not imagine that I have come to abolish the Law or the Prophets. I have come not to abolish but to complete them." (Matthew 5:17)

12 Liturgy, from the Greek *laos*, meaning "people," and *ergon*, meaning "work," "performance," "expression." Liturgy is not about individuals. It concerns itself with a community's self-identity and sense of mission. The individualistic nature of Western society is a culture hostile to good liturgy and may explain in great part our current struggle to be relevant.

13 Humans resort to using symbols when ordinary language fails. Symbolic language is the most real form of language we possess–yet how frequently we hear the comment, "Is it *only symbolic*"?

14 The very word "blood" is difficult for contemporary Western people. Some see it as crude and overly graphic for their sensibilities. Carl Jung commented on our inability to be comfortable with primal symbolic language. Yet without the language of symbol, how can we ever communicate the "reasons of the heart"? In religious traditions, some words–and "blood" is one of them–are simply too pregnant with layers of meaning to be easily jettisoned. Our task is to reconnect with tradition and early wisdom.

15 In the Gospels, when speaking of the wine at the Last Supper, Mark and Matthew use the simple words: "This is my blood, the blood of the covenant ... " (Mark 14:24, Matthew 26:28). Luke differs by adding the word "new" before covenant (Luke 22:20). St. Paul, in 1

Corinthians 11:25, also inserts the crucial word "new" before covenant. The Church continues this use of "new" at each Mass.

16 In drinking from the cup, sensibilities must be taken into consideration. Out of love, those who are sick should refrain. Perhaps more hygienic methods of sharing the cup–while still retaining the perception that we are drinking of the same commitment–can be developed.

Chapter 2

1 Habakkuk 2:1.

2 There are two ways of talking about Jesus, two sets of language. One is called a *high Christology* (as in the Gospel of John), the other a *low Christology* (as in the Gospels of Matthew Mark and Luke). The religious congregation to which I belong has a tradition of favoring the low approach, which emphasizes the human dimensions of Jesus' life. In the human, the divine emerges. We know and are familiar with the human side of Jesus (and of ourselves); we *believe* in the divine dimension that was revealed to us thereby–the divine aspect of Jesus and also (through him) of humanity.

3 Matthew paints an unflattering portrait of the Jewish leaders and Pharisees. We have come to realize that he paints them *as he knew them at the time of writing the Gospel*–probably around the year eighty (fifty or so years after Jesus lived and died). The hostility at that time between Jews and Christians (who were former Jews) is well recorded; it was one reason for Matthew writing in the first place.

4 In Hebrew prayer, the personal pronouns "me, my, I" stand principally for the nation; when Jewish people prayed the Psalms, they were prayed on behalf of the people. This tradition is maintained in *The Prayer of the Church*: when members of the Church pray the Psalms each day they are giving voice to all of humanity, and even all of creation.

5 Perhaps these, like treasured phrases, were all of each Psalm that Jesus prayed. Or perhaps they represent his struggle to sing each Psalm in its entirety–we will never know. But clearly the 150 Psalms were Jesus' prayerbook, loved and learned by heart. Their language and images fashioned his mind and fired his vision. So habitual had they become, and so precious a part of his consciousness, that they fill his mind on the Cross in those final moments of consciousness.

6 The full text, used as the first reading of the Mass on the first Sunday of the Passion, provides a vivid portrayal of the way Jesus would live: "Morning by morning he makes *my ear alert, to listen like a disciple*. Lord Yahweh has *opened my ear* ... "

7 The fullness of God, the flowering of the hidden self, is the motif of Paul's beautiful prayer for his churches in Ephesians 3:14-21.

8 See Acts 11:1-18 and Paul's own considered account in Galatians 2.

9 The Eucharist is not the preserve of the already holy. Despite one aspect of our traditional mindset that demanded purity of heart and conscience (that is, through Confession) prior to any reception of Communion, the Gospels remind us that the Eucharist is a way of salvation for strugglers. If the community is inclusive and loving, why not its rituals of celebration?

10 *Hamartia* is composed of two parts: ha is the attachment at the front of a word that indicates a negative: "not." From archery comes the Greek word for a target: *martia*. To be "on target" is *martia*; to be "off target" is *ha-martia*. Our usage of "to miss the point" seems very close.

Chapter 3

1 From the marriage song "Bound in Truth," in the collection *Kindly Light*.

2 I assume the convention of calling the author of this first Gospel by the name of Mark. Like all the Gospels, the naming of the author probably reflects more that this important collection of stories was compiled within a circle of churches that reflected a tradition of faith now associated with this Gospel's thrust and focus–that is, churches "with a Marcan flavor." It is simply easier to refer to the author as "Mark."

3 Internal evidence suggests strongly that Mark wrote toward the end of the sixties for a mixed community of Jewish and non-Jewish believers (possibly located in Rome) which was experiencing much pressure to stay faithful. Their Jewish linkage-in-faith was possibly being shaken by the Roman assault on Jerusalem and the Roman persecution of the Church's leadership (Peter). They needed desperately to maintain the purity of their inherited Jewish rituals–especially the Eucharist.

4 Exodus 18:13-26. The people of God are organized into manageable groupings of thousands, hundreds, fifties, and tens. Moses is advised to choose from the people at large some capable and God-fearing men (sic), trustworthy and incorruptible, and appoint them as leaders of the people.

5 These related stories may represent two slightly altered accounts of the one event in Jesus' life. Oral stories have a way of reshaping themselves in the telling and according to the audience. The changes may thus be accidental, or Mark may have made them deliberately. The second story, omitting references to Hebrew tradition (the Exodus and the number twelve), may represent an edited version for non-Jewish churches.

6 The second story is located in a section which describes Jesus as moving outside Galilee: to the territory of Tyre (Mark 7:24), thence by way of Sidon and through the Decapolis region–the ten cities (Mark 7:31)–to the setting of the second feeding story, and thence on to the region of Dalmanutha (Mark 8:10). For Jesus, this represents a significant journey out beyond the boundaries of Jewish culture and influence.

7 See Luke 22:19 and Paul in 1 Corinthians 11:24-25. Interestingly, Paul would have written his piece before the Gospels of Mark, Luke, and Matthew were written–and yet Mark and Matthew do not mention the phrase, "Do this in memory of me."

8 From the Third Eucharistic Prayer, immediately after the Consecration. This merging of identity with Jesus is the point of Christian faith. It is the core meaning of Baptism, Eucharist and Communion. This Third Eucharistic Prayer was constructed after Vatican II to blend the best of differing traditions of Eastern and Western Catholicism and to express the ideal of Christian holiness.

9 All Gospel versions of this miracle are constructed around this same pattern. Any slight variations (additions or omissions) between the Gospel writers are there to make other significant points that reflect major themes related to the needs of the communities for which they were writing. This is especially true of Luke who names as an integral part of the story the crowd's need for *lodging* as well as *food*. Lodging is important in Luke's portrayal of Jesus' life–and the Church's life–as a *journey*.

10 Data on this apparently common practice in the early Church is not plentiful, but St. Cyprian (d. 258) is quoted as criticizing those "who come without an offering but nonetheless take part of the sacrifice which the poor person has provided" (*De Opere et Eleemosynis*, 15). In other words, they have come forward for Communion and are thus consuming some of the bread and wine that they themselves have not provided. Hippolytus, writing in the church of Rome in the early third century, also mentions the practice.

11 "Carried forward" is the meaning of the original Latin combination *ob-ferre*, thus "of-ferre" or "offering" in English, and hence, the older term "the Offertory." In a sense it is truly "an offering," but to the poor (that is, to God). Later practice would shift this fine shade of meaning into simply, "we offer our gifts to God," confusing this aspect of the ritual with the prayers of offering after the Consecration. By the time this began to happen (in the Middle Ages), the congregation were no longer participating in any procession of gifts, but were rather a silent, non-involved audience to a drama about Jesus that was happening on the altar. Nor, by that time, did the congregation generally participate in Communion.

This confusion around the word "offertory" prompted the reformers of Vatican II to rename this action *Preparation of Gifts*. The "offering to God" occurs within the Eucharistic Prayer. One can only note that once the people lost their rightful involvement in the ritual of this procession of gifts, the whole meaning of "the offering" became obscured, even missed altogether.

12 *Apologia* I, 67 (as translated in the *Catechism of the Catholic Church*, no. 1351). By the time of Hippolytus of Rome (c.170-c.236), such gifts were blessed after the Eucharist was concluded. In those times there was no one way of celebrating the Eucharist–although the basic elements were uniform. Traditions varied slightly from location to location, from culture to culture.

The bishop took care of *all in need*. In today's church situation, perhaps those *in need* would include the general pastoral concerns of the parish itself. Collections of generosity in Paul's time were made for the welfare of the Jerusalem church. The Church itself, of course, may also be *in need*.

13 This gathering of gifts happened in different ways in different localities–sometimes it seems to have occurred prior to the celebration, with only the deacons being then involved in *bringing them forward*. However, the outline presented here is representative enough of the broad sweep of the differing traditions in the East and West.

14 Older Catholics will remember that the washing of hands by the priest had become a prayerful gesture of purification from sin. Many prayers that became part of the Roman Mass during the Middle Ages concerned themselves with such appeals for forgiveness, known as prayers of apology. Vatican II removed most of them in its attempt to return to the best of Roman tradition.

15 Jesus, obviously, but also ourselves. This play upon the deeper meanings of words is typical of all good liturgy. Educating the broader Church into the existence of such layered meaning is one task today. The rituals of the Church–its sacraments–are highly poetic constructions. Literalism (recognizing only one meaning to a word or gesture) has no place in Christian liturgy.

16 This is but one example of the Consecration Acclamations. A variety of such acclamations are now available to communities. They are all carefully constructed around *past, present*, and *future* tense verbs.

17 Is it no wonder that local communities, led by insightful presiders, are increasingly joining in the third of these acclamations (by law reserved to the priest). It is as if the people are sensing their rights–they share, after all, the first two of these important acclamation moments. An "Amen" is often just not good enough; an "Amen" repeated endlessly can be worse. Why not let the people share the substance of the prayer; the priest is still *presiding*.

18 *Epiclesis* is a Greek word, made up of two parts: *epi-* meaning "down"; and *klesis* meaning "a calling."

19 Some traditions have two such Epiclesis prayers, notably our Roman tradition. Others, especially in the Eastern tradition, have only one. What is important to note is this: in our Roman tradition, the first Epiclesis Prayer (before the Consecration) calls the Spirit down onto the *gifts*; the second Epiclesis Prayer (after the Consecration) asks for the *community to be now filled* by that same Spirit.

Where the Eastern Churches use only the one Epiclesis Prayer, the underlying thought is to ask the Spirit down onto the *gifts* which, once received in Communion, will in turn fill *the community* with that same Spirit.

In either tradition the outcome is the same: a Spirit-filled community who *become* the presence of Christ.

20 Eucharistic Prayer III.

21 Eucharistic Prayer III. The Epiclesis prayers of the early Church were not greatly dissimilar.

22 Sadly, we are cautious of the word *symbol*. Our culture treats it to mean something *not quite real*, when in fact the opposite is the case. The term comes from the Greek, a conjunction of two terms: *sum-* meaning "alongside," and *ballo* meaning "to place" or "throw." Thus, a "symbol" is used to express what might otherwise be difficult to convey: in this case, to convey adequately that we wish to give our whole being to God by living for others. By using the *symbol* of *a gift destined for the poor*, we make obvious to all what might otherwise be inexpressible. When the *symbol* is then consecrated to become *the reality called Jesus*, we ourselves are contained in that act of consecration.

23 One important document of the third century, from Rome, stresses the connection between the two processions. Hippolytus, in his *Apostolic Tradition* (n.20), written about 215, notes that only those could bring forward gifts (*offerre*) who were in communion with the Church and could therefore receive the bread back when it had been changed.

24 We *dare* to pray the "Our Father." The word is no exaggeration, but is a literal translation of the older Latin word with which the presider introduced the prayer in the Tridentine rite: *audemus dicere*: "let us dare to pray." The community committed in love to humanity is the Lord today. *We* redeem, *we* intercede, *we* incarnate the *hesed* and *emet* of God.

25 The Sign of Peace was not always placed at this point. Indeed, until restored to the community in the reform of Vatican II, it had dropped out of usage entirely (except between ministers at High Mass). In earlier times it had been located differently, but even when employed right after the liturgy of the Word (to lock the Word into our hearts), it was still, in a sense, a signature to the new covenant of obedience to the Word.

26 In past times, we were not alert to the discrepancy that while *breads* could be taken from the tabernacle, *wine* could not. (cf. General Instruction of Roman Missal, n.56)

27 Outstretched hands–whether in giving eucharistic gifts or receiving them–now seems quite an integral eucharistic gesture. Reception on the tongue is out of eucharistic character.

28 In the language of faith, a *mystery* is something *into which we have been lifted*. Its origin lies in the Greek word *mysterion*, and in the *mystery religions* of that pre-Christian culture. The Church later appropriated this specialist term to itself when speaking of the sacraments (but especially of the Eucharist).

Chapter 4

1 From the song "The Cross of Christ," in the collection *Kindly Light*.

2 Obedience, from two Latin terms: *ob* meaning "right up against," and *audire* meaning "to listen." Jesus listened *right up against the realities* of his life. Our Western understanding of obedience as something submissive, as "doing what someone else has commanded," is wide of this basic, primary meaning. In the New Testament, obedience denotes an active, energetic, and dangerous engagement with life's issues.

3 Traditionally, this has come down to us in the theological terminology of transubstantiation. The Council of Trent's language concerning the Real Presence of Jesus will be more closely considered later in this chapter.

4 As previously noted, this phrase is also included by Paul in 1 Corinthians 11:24, but in neither Mark or Matthew. I have used the text here as if spoken by Jesus himself (and perhaps it was). The insight still holds, however, even if such a redefining from Exodus to Jesus was performed by the early Church reflecting on his life and writing that understanding back into the "accounts" of the Last Supper.

5 Gestures, rituals, and words must be *sincere*. Sincerity is the basis of all social trust. It is a Latin word made of two parts: *sine-* meaning "without," and *cera* meaning "wax"; a sincere word is one "without wax," with nothing coming between speaker and hearer. One task in worship today is to render the rituals *sine-ceras*, so that they become accessible to all concerned.

6 The term *insincere* is a double negative: *in-* meaning "not," and (as we have seen) *sine-cera* meaning "without wax." Hence to be *in-sine-cera* means to be "not without interfering wax," that is, to be unclear.

7 John's eucharistic language is found in chapter six. Scholars differ on how eucharistic the language was intended to be–yet the Church uses images from this writing constantly when speaking of the Eucharist (flesh, food, blood, drink, eternal life).

8 Foot washing was a sign of hospitality common in cultures of the time. See especially Abraham's hospitality in Genesis 18:4; Abigail's welcome for David's servants in 1 Samuel 25:41; and the woman who washes Jesus' feet in Luke 7:44. Hospitality was the transparent meaning of such a gesture. Unfamiliar to us, we can miss this dimension of hospitality, mistaking it for a mere gesture of cleanliness.

9 The overtones of washing will later be read as baptismal language by the Church. In those days, of course, baptism and the Eucharist were considered as the one event, received on the one night of Easter, a complete process of initiation. The interplay between baptismal and eucharistic images should not surprise us.

10 "The Jews" is generally understood today as a generic phrase for those opposing belief in Jesus. It is not the blanket reference to the Jewish people that many of us once supposed it to be, with the dangerous anti-Semitic overtones that can follow.

11 The Council of Trent uses a range of words to grapple with the realism of the eucharistic presence of Jesus: "the *whole* Christ is *truly*, *really*, and *substantially* contained [in the sacrament]." Quoted in the recent *Catechism of the Catholic Church* (no. 1374), this important Tridentine text also uses the celebrated phrasing, "the body and blood, together with the *soul* and *divinity* [of Christ]." The Church has employed a range of images to give adequate expression to the *depth of mystery* we know the Eucharist to be.

12 Just as the Roman military oath of allegiance to the Emperor (the *sacramentum*) totally changed forever the recruit's relationship to the Emperor, can we not say that the sacrament celebrating *the presence of Jesus* (and engaged in by all present) *totally* and *forever changes* our

relationship with Jesus? Such a presence, creating such an experienced effect in our lives, could well be described as *substantial, real, whole* and *entire*.

13 *Summa Theologiae*, IIIa, 76, 5.

14 In the *Catechism of the Catholic Church* (no. 1374), the Church is searching for the richest language in which to speak about the presence of Jesus. Explaining there the meaning of "real," we find these traditional references: "it is a *substantial* presence" by which Christ is "*wholly* and *entirely* present." Beautiful is the belief that *everything that makes Jesus the person he is* (his mission, reality and being) remains totally accessible to us and is portrayed in this celebration we call Eucharist. Whatever we understand by the presence of Christ, it must be read in terms of its meaning for us. St. Augustine makes this point strongly (in *Enarrationes in Psalmos*, 98.9), when he imagines Jesus explaining the meaning of sacrament to his disciples: Understand what I have said *spiritually*. You will not eat *this body that you see*, nor will you drink *the blood that will be shed by those who crucify me*. A *sacrament* is what I have given you: *understood spiritually*, it will give you life.

15 Our sacramental language with children, and adults, needs care. Understandings that function when we are young must be developed in step with maturity, otherwise we find adults trying to live adult life with childishly undeveloped religious images–a recipe for disaster.

16 The Church emphasises that the priest presiding at Eucharist speaks for the assembled congregation: the priest stands in the person of Christ the Head (of the Body). This celebrated phrase (Latin: *in persona Christi capitis*) forms the core of her teaching in Catechism nos. 1548-1553.

17 Written sometime between 52 and 58 (around 25 years after the death of Jesus), this is our earliest written reference to the Eucharist and contains a few important comments relating to how the Corinthians were celebrating the Lord's Supper.

Chapter 5

1 From the song "The Cross of Christ," in the collection *Kindly Light*. In John's Gospel, the glory of God is most manifest as Jesus dies on the Cross. To stand in the shadow of that glory is our baptismal commitment. The first ritual of baptism is the tracing of the Cross on the forehead of the recipient.

2 By the time of Vatican II, the Mass was overloaded with prayers and gestures (signs of the Cross, genuflections, purification prayers) whose origins lay in the Germanic cultures of the Middle Ages. The reform of Vatican II removed most of them. Even a gesture such as the washing of hands by the priest–originally connected with Hebrew ritual and then becoming an important (and necessary) element in the early Church's Procession of Gifts–in the Middle Ages was provided with a new meaning: cleansing from sin. The gesture had endured but its original meaning had been hijacked.

3 The fruit of all true prayer is this capacity to *notice* what is going on around us. It is a prayerfulness that matures in silence.

4 From the prayers of the priest at the Preparation of the Gifts in the eucharistic liturgy. These prayers over bread and wine–deliberately *berakah*–have been carefully modeled on Jewish table prayers.

5 Isaiah 52:13-53:12 is the first reading from the Good Friday liturgy. Its powerful image of the Suffering Servant was applied by the Church to Jesus. It speaks of an untimely death, an unfinished life. Unless we recover this uncompleted dimension to the life of Jesus, we fail to appreciate the total humanness that he took to himself. Some insist that Jesus had completed his full agenda at the time of his death, maintaining that the Church has no power to address issues that Jesus did not address in his limited life span (or culture). Surely this is a misreading of the mystery of the Incarnation.

6 Eucharist is composed of two Greek terms: *eu-* meaning "well"; and *karis* meaning "grace," "favor," "kindness"–hence meanings for us of well-graced, well-favored, blessed, or kindly dealt with. From this flows the popular sense of "giving thanks for the graciousness received." One can immediately see the value of such a name for our Sunday celebration over the previous opaque term "the Mass." Another source of difficulty for some is the expression "the sacrifice of the Mass" that can miss the sense of *berakah* behind the response of Jesus to lay down his life. We must recapture the joy under the sacrifice, or we will miss its truly Christian dimension.

7 Terms like "Consecration" and "the Mass" have been replaced (since Vatican II) with terminology both more descriptive and

more faithful to earlier traditions: "the Narrative of Institution" (the Last Supper references) and, for the Mass, "the Eucharist." When discussing issues of worship, our use of such terms is still in transition and both sets of terms continue to be used.

8 Three major congregational acclamations now punctuate all forms of the Eucharist Prayer: the Preface Acclamation ("Holy, holy, holy Lord ... "), the Great Acclamation after the Narrative of Institution (e.g. "Christ has died! Christ has risen! Christ will come again!"), and the Acclamation Amen in response to the final Doxology of the priest ("Through him, with him, in him ... "). As well, there are continuing attempts to develop musical forms of this lengthy prayer, constructed around further, more regular interventions on the part of the congregation. The Church is cautious about such developments as they represent an exploration of the delicate interplay between priest and people–and issues of priesthood (or community leadership) are of great sensitivity and traditional significance.

9 Over eighty different Preface texts are presented in the current Roman Missal, yet only some dozen or so texts of the Eucharistic Prayer proper have been approved. This reflects the particular Roman tradition of letting the variable Preface provide the local color to a feast while maintaining the uniqueness and theological integrity of the one Roman Canon (Eucharistic Prayer I) throughout history.

10 From the *Apostolic Tradition* of Hippolytus of Rome, confidently attributed to around the year 215. This lengthy document, a treasure-trove of liturgical rituals and practice in the Roman churches of the time, is nevertheless an intricate and debated piece of writing. It is safe to say that while declaring to speak of the traditions of the Roman Church, its origins lie in the churches of the Eastern Mediterranean, perhaps in Egyptian Alexandria. Nevertheless, the richness and detail of its portrayal of ritual is so significant that Vatican II scholars were more than happy to model the new Eucharistic Prayer II upon it–albeit with some careful alterations to wording and structure to give it a more Roman appearance.

11 If using the present tense like this is so educational for the congregation, why not *always* make use of it in the Preface? Why maintain the slip from present to past and back again to present tense? Once people become "tense aware," the retention of past tense is no longer a disadvantage because it does link our consciousness with the historical story of Jesus. As long as we are not fooled into reading it as *merely* an historical reference, the linkage to the past is crucial in ritual. However, for reasons of education in ritual thinking, an *occasional* use of the present tense format would seem helpful.

12 In Greek, *mysterion*. Note that the term does not primarily refer to something beyond our understanding (as in mysterious), except in this precise sense: by participating in the ritual we are taken onto a plane of existence (and meaning) that would otherwise be "beyond us." The ritual confers on our lives a mysterious (yet deeply appreciated) perspective: almost a "new life."

13 It is this sense of "complete participation" (*Catechism of the Catholic Church*, no. 1372) that is the crux of eucharistic understanding. The *Catechism* here quotes St. Augustine with pride: "The Church continues to reproduce this sacrifice [of Jesus] in the sacrament of the altar ... wherein it is evident ... that *in what she offers she herself is offered*." Earlier the *Catechism* stresses the tradition that there is only "one single sacrifice" (no. 1367) and that this perception alone makes it possible "for all generations of Christians to be united with his offering" (no. 1368). It continues: "Like Christ who stretched out his arms on the cross, *through him, with him*, and *in him, she offers herself* and intercedes for all men [sic]."

14 Eucharistic Prayer III, the Memorial Prayer immediately after the Great Acclamation.

15 From the Greek terms *doxa*, meaning "teaching," and *logos*, meaning "word" (or "expression"). In this sense, the doxology is "the summary of the teaching." Into the words of this brief prayer is packed an immense theological understanding.

16 Surely the presidential role of the priest is not lost when the presider leads the assembly in a shared (and sung) Acclamation.

17 It is a term with two elements: *ana-*, meaning "forwards," and *mnesis*, meaning "remember." Thus the *anamnesis* does not simply mean to look backwards in memory of something, but rather to bring that past event forwards into the present moment–not an easy concept for us today. But note how close the word is to describing the interplay between the past, the present, and the future which is the crux of all liturgical ritual.

Chapter 6

1 From the song "The Cross of Christ," in the collection *Kindly Light*.

2 While this is generally true of the readings, there are some exceptions: for example, in the Sundays after Easter the first reading is taken from the Acts of the Apostles and portrays the growth of the early Church. But St. Augustine's oft repeated aphorism provides the general format when the Church chooses its readings for liturgy: "The New Testament lies hidden in the Old; the Old Testament comes fully to light in the New" (as quoted in the General Introduction to the Lectionary, no. 5).

3 "The word of God is something alive and active: it cuts more incisively than any two-edged sword: it can seek out the place where soul is divided from spirit, or joints from marrow; it can pass judgement on secret emotions and thoughts. No created thing is hidden from him; everything is uncovered ... " (Hebrews 4:12-13).

4 Such pondering is usually associated with personal, private prayer. Unless such prayer propels us toward others, toward community and service, it cannot be of the Spirit. In one sense, therefore, the primary prayer-form of the Church is its liturgy, done in common with others. All other forms of prayer lead to it, or are extensions of it.

5 Luke 24:35. The "breaking of bread" is a technical term in the early Church for the Eucharist. Whatever Luke intended to convey by this Emmaus story, he certainly has something crucial about the eucharistic ritual in mind.

6 This strong quotation from Vatican II's *Constitution on the Liturgy* (no.56) is written into the General Introduction to the Lectionary (no.10).

7 In those days, even lateness for Mass was judged by whether one was in time for the Offertory; the readings and all that went before were seen as merely preparatory for the sacrifice. One could also be excused for leaving early (!) as long as one remained until the *priest* had received communion. The fractured nature of the pre-Vatican II ritual should be kept in mind when appreciating the current task of generating full participation in the ritual. The so-called tradition out of which we have so recently emerged was far more wounded, far more fragmented, than we like to remember.

8 The term "*sacrifice*" is all too easily understood in a pagan way. Even in the Bible it can be so found: Abraham was going to sacrifice (i.e. kill) his son, Isaac, as an offering to a demanding God. As Hebrew faith developed, this pagan sense of sacrifice was refined into a submission of the human spirit before the demands of love. In Psalm 40 we read:

> You wanted no sacrifice ... ,
> but you gave me an open ear,
> you did not ask for burnt offering or
> sacrifice for sin; then I said, "Here am I, I
> am coming." (40:6-7)

This was the sacrifice seen in Jesus: an obedience to love that eventually caused his death.

9 *Constitution on the Liturgy*, no. 14.

10 In Greek, *martyrion* means "to give witness." Martyrs are seen as giving exemplary witness to the Story of Jesus: loving as he loved, dying as he died. In this they were seen as embodiments of the eucharistic commitment.

11 This is a foundational text, frequently commented upon by the early Fathers and used constantly in Church documents to describe the meaning of Christian sacrifice. It has been written deliberately into the text of Eucharistic Prayer III:

> From age to age you gather a people to
> yourself, so that *from east to west*
> *a perfect offering* may be made
> to the glory of your name.

12 The "pure offering" of Malachi became in the Greek of the early Church the *logike thusia*, from *logike*, meaning "rational," "involving our rational capacities," and *thusia*, meaning "sacrifice." Ambrose of Milan (c.339-397) translated this into Latin as *sacrificium rationabilis*, "the sacrifice of our spirits" ("spiritual sacrifice"). Gregory the Great (c.540-604), in his reform of the Roman Liturgy, is thought to have slightly altered the meaning of *sacrificium rationabilis* to "reasonable sacrifice" (that

is, the appropriate, or even acceptable sacrifice).

Following Malachi 1:11, and reflecting the above path of development, we find in Eucharistic Prayer IV:

We offer you his body and blood, the *acceptable sacrifice* which brings salvation to the whole world.

In today's debate about whether the Eucharist is "a sacrifice" or a "meal," clear understandings of the tradition of Christian sacrifice (from Malachi through to the usage in the Roman Eucharistic Prayers) are very important. A pagan understanding of sacrifice is of no help to us.

13 Creation is very much part of the eucharistic celebration. Bread and wine are representative of much more than the people gathered for the celebration. Listen to the prayers we speak over them:

Blessed are you, Lord, God of all creation. Through your goodness we have *this bread* [and wine] to offer, which earth has given and human hands have made.

It will become for us the bread of life [and our spiritual drink].

Until we begin to sense the sacred dimensions of *all* food, *all* drink, *all* people, and *all* creation, we will remain impoverished in our awareness of what constitutes the core of the eucharistic celebration.

14 General Introduction to the Lectionary, no. 47. The flow from Word, through the following sacramental gesture, and on into our lives is one simple movement of meaning. To recapture this simplicity is today's liturgical task. Presiders and all who minister during the Eucharist must possess this vision and sense of flow into life. Without this unified imagination, ministers–especially those who preside–create blockages within the process.

15 The *presider's* role in the preliminary rites should prepare the congregation toward the focus of the Gospel Reading. Without carefully managed preparation (and presentation), the Word might otherwise easily pass them by. How to carry elements of the Word forward into the Eucharistic Prayer will be dealt with later.

16 Not everything in a piece of Scripture is of equal importance. All a reader's craft is needed to emphasize (without affectation) the point to be carried. There are many skills readers might acquire for doing this–it is a real ministry demanding the building of real skills. Not just anyone in a community possesses such skills. If the presider ministers each week, why cannot a commissioned group of readers minister each week? Without regular exposure and helpful feedback, how can the skills of our readership develop? Are too many involved in this sensitive ministry?

17 The Second Reading is frequently part of a continuing cycle through, for example, one of Paul's letters, with little actual bearing on the image of Jesus presented in the Gospel Reading. In times of heightened liturgy (Lent, Easter, Advent) the Second Reading is more carefully chosen to coordinate with the other two–but even then the complaint about the amount of Scripture being digested by an assembly still stands. The concern of those who crafted the Lectionary was that the brilliance of harmonizing the Old and New Testaments (in First Reading and Gospel) left the body of New Testament Letters aside. Hence, the establishment of the Second Reading cycle, lest the people be deprived of those New Testament treasures.

18 The General Instruction on the Roman Missal (henceforth GIRM), ch. 1, no. 2-3. The GIRM is not addressed directly to every local community, nor is it thereby an encouragement for localized initiatives involving a change to the structures of the ritual, but is rather a presentation of the thinking behind the already renewed liturgy. Yet the principles for liturgical renewal that drove Vatican II's vision must inform, surely, the local community's contemporary struggle to involve its people meaningfully in the ritual of the Eucharist. I make a point of these principles here so as to inform ourselves for the ongoing debate about the suitability of some elements within the current shape of the rite.

19 GIRM, ch. 1, no. 5. The emphasis on local discrimination is also interesting.

20 Such usage of segments outside the normal time for the Readings reinforces and imprints their message. We have to find creative ways to work the scriptures into the celebration: large blocks of impenetrable words are no longer sufficient. Again, the authority and pastoral experience of the GIRM (ch. 7, no. 313) speaks:

The pastoral effect of any celebration is enhanced if the readings, prayers, and chants are suited *as well as possible* to the needs, spiritual preparation, and receptivity of those who are to take part.

21 Nothing but our appreciation goes out to those who have generously borne the burden of readership over these initial years of renewal. They have carried us through a difficult transition and often at great personal cost to themselves. My point is more a structural one: advocating a systemic and developmental approach to readership ministry and some authoritative commissioning of readers that recognizes their importance for ministry in the wider Church. If it is indeed a *ministry*, then let us begin to treat it more professionally as a recognized and episcopally authorized *ministry*.

22 GIRM, ch. 3, no. 66, and quoted in the General Introduction to the Lectionary, no. 55.

23 General Introduction to the Lectionary, no. 28.

24 Should basic ecclesial communities take hold in a parish, such a structure might well effect the possible ways of celebrating the Word in any Sunday (whole parish) gathering. In such a structure, perhaps the neighborhood gatherings have already pondered and spoken the core of the Sunday Readings amongst themselves during the week, so that the Sunday celebration can feed off that prior experience of "silence" and "meditation" within the parish.

25 Lost, that is, except for the Bidding Prayers of Good Friday. The format of those ancient Good Friday prayers–stated intention, period of silence for personal prayer, short public prayer–remains the most useful model for our Prayers of the Faithful. All too frequently our prayers are verbose and busy, with little sense of silence and interiority.

26 Eucharistic Prayer II. One wonders when the rubric will encourage the assembly to be standing and singing the Acclamations and responses throughout the Eucharistic Prayer. For in the liturgy, standing was initially the symbol of resurrection and a readiness to live obediently the Word of God. Even more practically, singing is greatly enhanced when standing, notably diminished when attempted while kneeling.

Chapter 7

1 From "The Galilee Song".

2 Throughout history, the rituals of the liturgy have proven to be the Church's most effective instrument of adult faith formation. One is reminded of the wisdom of the saying: "When I hear, I forget; when I see, I remember; when I do, I understand." Truly involving rituals, reflecting sound theology, are still our most effective teaching process.

3 By "the poor" we mean that vast range of human need to which Jesus himself responded–all manner of sinners and social outcasts, the sick and imprisoned (in various ways), those whom Mark calls simply "the crowds". In short, all those elements of humanity and creation that call forth from us the compassion and tenderness of God.

4 The approval of a Eucharistic Prayer for Children greatly stimulated the revival of recurring sung responses for adult congregations as well. The history of liturgy indicates that once the Church approves an adaptation for one particular circumstance (in this case, for liturgy with children), then it has approved the wisdom of that adaptation in principle–and wider application is usually sure to follow. Notice that the need for such an adaptation came to the Church's awareness from concerned people involved with children. Unless we speak up, the Church remains unaware of such needs.

ABOUT THE AUTHOR

A Missionary of the Sacred Heart, Fr. Frank Andersen has studied spirituality and worship in Berkeley, California, and gained a Licentiate in Liturgy from the Pontifical Liturgical Institute of San Anselmo, Rome. He is well known throughout Australia for his retreats and adult faith-education work. He has been involved in parish formation and renewal programs, staff faith development, liturgical workshops, ministerial formation courses, and clergy renewal in-services. One of the most popular composers of modern hymns in Australia, Fr. Andersen's collections include *Eagle's Wings, Everything I Possess, Rising Moon,* and *Kindly Light.* His first book, *Jesus: Our Story,* was a religious bestseller in Australia and was published in both America (as *Imagine Jesus...*) and Europe. His work in recent years, as part of a team engaged in adult faith formation, has involved him in diocesan, parish and staff programs throughout Australia.